The
COMPASSIONATE
SAMURAI

Also by Brian Klemmer

EATING THE ELEPHANT ONE BITE AT A TIME:
52 Weekly Lessons in Leadership

IF HOW-TO'S WERE ENOUGH, WE WOULD ALL BE
SKINNY, RICH & HAPPY

WHEN GOOD INTENTIONS RUN SMACK INTO REALITY:
Twelve Lessons to Coach Yourself and Others to Peak Performance

Hay House Titles of Related Interest

YOU CAN HEAL YOUR LIFE, the movie,
starring Louise L. Hay & Friends
(available as a 1-DVD program and an expanded 2-DVD set)
Watch the trailer at: **www.LouiseHayMovie.com**

THE SHIFT, the movie,
starring Dr. Wayne W. Dyer
(available as a 1-DVD program and an expanded 2-DVD set)
Watch the trailer at: **www.DyerMovie.com**

FOUR ACTS OF PERSONAL POWER: How to Heal Your Past and
Create a Positive Future, by Denise Linn

THE TIMES OF OUR LIVES: Extraordinary True Stories of
Synchronicity, Destiny, Meaning, and Purpose,
by Louise L. Hay & Friends

YOU CAN HAVE WHAT YOU WANT: Proven Strategies
for Inner and Outer Success, by Michael Neill

All of the above are available at your local bookstore, or may be
ordered by visiting: Hay House USA: **www.hayhouse.com®**; Hay House
Australia: **www.hayhouse.com.au**; Hay House UK: **www.hayhouse**
.co.uk; Hay House South Africa: **www.hayhouse.co.za**;
Hay House India: **www.hayhouse.co.in**

The
COMPASSIONATE
SAMURAI

BEING EXTRAORDINARY
IN AN ORDINARY WORLD

BRIAN KLEMMER

HAY HOUSE, INC.

Carlsbad, California • New York City
London • Sydney • Johannesburg
Vancouver • Hong Kong • New Delhi

Library of Congress Cataloging No.: 2007935332

Tradepaper ISBN: 978-1-4019-2045-6
Digital ISBN: 978-1-4019-2104-0

14 13 12 11   15 14 13 12
1st edition, January 2008
12th edition, February 2011

Printed in the United States of America

This book is dedicated to all the real-life compassionate samurai who are ethically leading lives with boldness to create a world that works for everyone, with no one left out. This book is also dedicated to all the compassionate samurai who have gone before us and have given so much, including their lives, so that we could be privileged to carry the cause forward.

CONTENTS

INTRODUCTION

I want this book to awaken a resonance in you like a tuning fork that vibrates so much that it compels you to take extreme action. In general, people fall into one of two categories: They're either kind, caring individuals who can't make anything happen; or they're heartless, self-centered jerks with no values who make big things happen.

Think about your days in high school. It might be a stretch, but just reminisce for a minute. Who dated the best-looking girls? Many times, wasn't it the boorish jocks with the most offensive attitudes and careless manners? On the other hand, the nicest, kindest, most considerate guys couldn't get a girlfriend. Who dated the best-looking guys? Wasn't it often the girls with fairly loose standards?

Look in the newspaper at the endless stream of greedy, unethical people from Tyco International, Arthur Andersen, and Enron who raked in unbelievable amounts of cash, were convicted of fraud, and ended up in jail. Unfortunately, they had no compassion for the people whose lives they ruined in the process. Think about the top executives in the tobacco industry who denied the obvious health implications associated with smoking. And how many jokes have you heard that lampoon attorneys because so many have more regard for profit than justice?

We often hear the expression "Nice guys finish last" (this isn't gender specific). The compassionate guy with the big heart never seems to get what he wants in life, while the rude one always seems to achieve his desires. Tragically, many of us accept this paradigm as the way life should be and as an acceptable way for people to behave. For the most part, we tend to believe (whether we want to admit it or not) that truly good-hearted people will never make a whole lot of money, be influential, or achieve the honors they deserve in life.

Intuitively, we don't believe that compassionate individuals make a tangible difference. This is a global problem; it doesn't just exist in the United States. It's the reason why corruption is rampant in developing countries. Selfish people with their dog-eat-dog mentality seem to enjoy a crème de la crème lifestyle. Many people believe that a cutthroat attitude is necessary in order to achieve the very best. I've written this book to let you know that you can be a mover and a shaker in the business or political world, enjoy great relationships and the finer things in life, and still be a caring person.

If you look carefully, there are many examples of this type of individual throughout history, in all cultures and in all walks of life. The ones who come to mind include General Robert E. Lee, the American Civil War Confederate leader; Saladin, the Muslim warrior of the 12th-century Crusades; and Nelson Mandela, the anti-apartheid activist and former president of South Africa. It's very possible for you, too, to become what I've dubbed the "compassionate samurai."

The samurai were members of a Japanese warrior caste that rose to power in the 12th-century and dominated the government until 1868. They were famous as the most feared and respected warriors of their day and were known for being stoic and totally unfazed by circumstances. The warriors lived according to a very strict code of values—later known as *Bushido*—that emphasized bravery, honor, and personal loyalty.

Bushido literally means "the way of the warrior." The very concept of a samurai with a kindhearted side seems oxymoronic, yet the word *samurai* means "to serve." In essence, the heart of such a person is to help others. So I've stretched this aspect in coining the term *compassionate samurai* to mean someone with strong values who can absolutely make anything happen and yet whose whole life is about service.

With this balance, I believe that you can achieve extraordinary relationships, advance to the top of your career, enjoy financial prosperity, and contribute to others in a significant way while enjoying inner personal satisfaction. The balance of warrior and compassion is perhaps the most perfect union, combining the enjoyment of outward success with a feeling of integrity and peace.

No matter what area you desire to succeed in, use this book as a working guide to help you embrace the concept of living to help others win in life. WorldCom, Arthur Andersen, and Enron would still be thriving corporations if their executives had read an advance copy of *The Compassionate Samurai* and integrated it into their corporate culture.

Excitement may create momentum, but *character is the only thing that lasts*. Show me a company, a country, or an individual without character, and I will show you a fleeting entity. This is what concerns me today about the United

States. We're suffering from an erosion of character. If we aren't careful, the effects will be like a massive mudslide swiftly headed toward destruction rather than the slow wearing away of a rock.

The enormous prosperity we've enjoyed as a result of our forefathers' character is in jeopardy of vanishing. We're concerned with our immediate financial income as the future of our children's social security fades away. Some parents respond to the problem of the quality of education these days by enrolling their kids in expensive private schools, while the public school system is reduced to a baby-sitting machine that produces students who are incapable of competing internationally.

The United States reactively funds prisons at a faster rate than any dictatorship, yet we won't get behind large-scale prevention programs. We allow the earth to be raped for whatever immediate profits companies can obtain. The anti-American sentiment that exists in many parts of the world isn't simply a product of the haves versus the have-nots, although that jealousy certainly exists. It's the juxtaposition of the incredible prosperity that they desperately want served with blatant disregard for others.

Don't think that I'm bashing the United States. I love my country, but I'm sounding a trumpet call to resurrect our greatness, sending forth the message that what works for you individually can also be effective nationally and internationally. The compassionate samurai doesn't seek his own interest. He firmly believes in serving others even if that means that he must sacrifice himself in the process. Please don't mistake this as being a martyr. The willingness to give doesn't mean living from the place of deprivation.

Nearly every organization has dominant, take-charge people. Unfortunately, they're quite often the most negative, self-centered employees. I don't want to create wimps out of them. My objective is to show them that they don't have to be poor leaders who pursue their interests at the expense of others. Dominant individuals can still win as they help those around them succeed. However it may seem, cold, calloused attitudes aren't the formula for success in the world of commerce.

On the other hand, people who have caring hearts but who lack the courage to accomplish results are also self-centered. They're simply hiding their insecurities with a noble cloak. The truth is, they care more about their comfort than the suffering of others. This attitude leads to becoming judgmental, yet not accountable to anyone. My objective is also to help these compassionate souls tap into their warrior nature so that they, too, can win battles in life and not be limited by their passive temperament.

In this book, I've listed ten codes that a compassionate samurai lives by: *commitment, personal responsibility, contribution, focus, honesty, honor, trust, abundance, boldness,* and *knowledge.* These traits make him a skilled warrior in battle as well as a compassionate fighter and creator. I'll elaborate on each trait in great detail, but understand that they aren't to be tried on every now and then—they must be practiced as a daily regimen until they become habitual.

You'll notice that all ten codes are character traits. What's exciting for you is that as you integrate them into your life, you'll have the potential for an exponential increase in your growth. Most books give information on how to do something—and that's not bad. But how-tos lead only to *incremental* increases; these are small, progressive steps toward change. Much greater, lasting shifts—or exponential alterations—occur when you actually change your character. For example, with a simple business model, you can make an incremental increase from this year to the next by simply working harder at what you're doing. By incorporating these ten character traits into your life, you'll create the opportunity for exponential, long-lasting transformation by leveraging good how-to's.

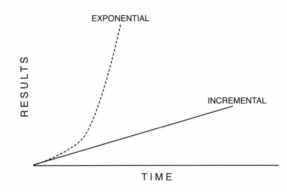

Most people believe that they have to choose: either riches without spirituality, or poverty and humility seasoned with the divine. You don't have to make this choice—you can have both! You can be rich and spiritual, wealthy and giving, a warrior in the marketplace—as well as a strong-willed, compassionate friend to many, including your family members and other loved ones. If you've ever had a challenge on either end of the spectrum—by demonstrating compassion toward others or by winning big battles in life (the true warrior within)—this book will show the way to strategically combine the two, making you the victor that you were always destined to be.

— **Brian Klemmer**, Klemmer & Associates

Author's Note: Throughout this book (and particularly in Chapter 11), I will present questions for you to answer. Please write down your answers on another piece of paper or in a journal.

Also, please note that a compassionate samurai can be either male or female; however, for literary simplicity, masculine pronouns are used within these pages.

Compassionate samurai say what
they mean and do what they say.
They make bold promises and keep them.

Average people do what they say
as long as it's convenient.

Chapter One

COMMITMENT

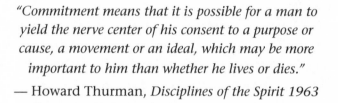

"Commitment means that it is possible for a man to yield the nerve center of his consent to a purpose or cause, a movement or an ideal, which may be more important to him than whether he lives or dies."
— Howard Thurman, *Disciplines of the Spirit 1963*

Talking about commitment usually evokes various responses. The compassionate samurai believes that it means doing what he says he's going to do. The average person believes in this concept . . . some of the time. He believes that he should do what he says he's going to when conditions are optimal or conducive for keeping his word. But honestly, commitment doesn't have conditions. A compassionate samurai follows through whether it feels good or not; average people do what they feel like doing.

The historical samurai kept their commitments even if it cost them their lives. It isn't that they didn't value themselves; it's just that they treasured keeping their word and principles more. Samurai were committed to uphold the tradition of honor, one of the ten traits I mentioned earlier. If one was killed because he upheld a principle such as keeping his word, then his death was honorable.

To a compassionate samurai, death isn't the worst thing that could happen. The greatest tragedy is to live either an unfulfilled life or one that lacks principles. The historical samurai would rather die than dishonor his name and the name of his calling.

Times have changed. For the most part, the average person today doesn't follow this line of thought. We live in a society that travels in practically the opposite direction. My goal—and that of this book and our Klemmer & Associates seminars—is to change the prevailing mind-set of our day.

The average person doesn't care about keeping his commitments, and the value of his word has become so cheap that he breaks it almost every day. Average salespeople promise things they can't deliver just to make a sale; average parents promise their children that they'll tuck them in or take them to the park, yet feel no remorse when they fail to follow through. Too many home-based entrepreneurs make unrealistic promises just to get clients—and as a result, the reputation of the whole industry suffers.

When average people are late for an appointment, they don't consider their tardiness to be a broken commitment. Divorce rates are extremely high. Corporate scandals are front-page news, long-standing friendships dissolve, personal debt forces many into bankruptcy, trust is lost forever, and people are afraid to do business with those who solicit them—all because of broken commitments. This list could go on for the rest of the chapter, but I think you've gotten the point: Commitment is the basis for trust, which is the foundation of all relationships. Therefore, breaking it equates to destroying trust.

When trust is broken, relationships inevitably become shaky. More than that, when commitments aren't valued and honored, the healthy process of both personal and business interactions and connections is turned upside down. When a person doesn't keep his promises, others don't want to do business with him or engage in personal relationships with him—and the "commitment breaker" becomes isolated. This costs huge amounts of money and time, destroying friendships, health, and pretty much anything else that really matters.

Quit Making Excuses—Just Say It and Do It

Many people make ridiculous excuses for why they don't want to commit. They are the *John Average Man* and the *Marianne Mediocre* of life. In a nutshell, commitment is doing what we say we're going to do. It's that simple. However, maybe we're getting ahead of ourselves. The average person doesn't have a problem doing what he says he's going to do—because he never says anything! He never commits himself.

Just think about the number of people you know who never make New Year's resolutions. Why do they shy away from it? It's because they're already invested in looking good by not breaking any promises. They're leading lives of convenience. However, the high price they pay is that they're never going to accomplish much of anything. They're giving up all their power because nothing happens without agreement. Unfortunately, there are a lot of individuals who enjoy this arrangement.

Do you want to be a compassionate samurai? If you do, you must make large agreements and keep your word. Life seems to work in proportion to the size of the promises we make and our ability to make good on them. If you're thinking about how you're going to follow through and be able to keep your word, bear with me; we'll get to that momentarily. First, you've got to say what you're going to do. Declare it without fear or doubt—or say it with fear and doubt, but make the statement anyway.

Now there are millions of people who resolve every New Year's Eve to lose weight, begin a new relationship, or even land a better-paying job. The majority of these well-wishers who wind up failing themselves aren't compassionate samurai. Those who are compassionate samurai get results and continue to stay motivated. Instead, discouragement settles in for the average people who fail to keep their New Year's resolutions.

Say what you're going to do. Declare it without fear
or doubt—or say it with fear and doubt, but
make the statement anyway.

When they don't lose weight, find that special someone, or get their promotion or raise, they throw in the towel. Instead of honestly reviewing the reason why they didn't achieve the goal (which is what a compassionate samurai would do), they trade in their positive confession and commitment for trite excuses. You've heard the average folks' lists of excuses exempting themselves from the possibility of winning in life. Maybe you've even used some of them a time or two.

- "I don't really need all that."

- "I'm not into having a lot of 'things'."

- "People who want the finest things in life are simply materialistic."

- "The key to happiness is to have no desires."

- "It's just God's will."

- "You can't be spiritual and have success."

- "Rich folks are greedy and don't have a heart of compassion for anyone."

The bottom line is that these are all excuses for not being where you want to be in life, not going to the places you were destined to go, and abandoning your responsibility to society. Mediocrity is the height of selfishness, and excuses are simply another way of being dishonest. Think about it: Yes, maybe there was traffic. But you could have gotten up earlier, or you could have told your mother that you didn't have time to talk with her at that moment because you had a commitment. Perhaps the truth wouldn't fly too well with the boss (or with yourself, really), so you make up an excuse.

Mediocrity is the height of selfishness.

5

Usually the excuse makes sense; it's reasonable. But now you're a slave to the tyranny of reason instead of enjoying the liberty brought about by results. Vince Lombardi, a famous American football coach, frequently told his players before a game: "In a few hours we'll all be back in here and you'll either have reasons or results. What is it going to be?" It's no accident that he coached Super Bowl championship teams. It didn't matter if it snowed or if their star quarterback broke his arm—those were just reasons. The players became compassionate samurai and were committed to results instead of being average and being reasonable.

Which are you going to choose? Average people make reasonable excuses for pretty much everything they fail to accomplish. This helps them gain acceptance, approval, understanding, and an exemption from ever having to try again. Sad to say, they give up the extraordinary life and results of a compassionate samurai. Commit to things that are meaningful to you because you were born to make a difference in life. The only way you'll ever see that coming to pass is when you start to make commitments.

In 1972 I graduated from the United States Military Academy, West Point. Within the first five minutes of entering the academy, we began to learn a valuable lesson. Our leaders taught us that we had only four answers to *any* question. No other response would be accepted or admissible. We were allowed to say:

1. "Yes, sir."
2. "No, sir."
3. "No excuse, sir."
4. "Sir, I do not understand."

If I were late to class, I could only give one of those four answers. It didn't matter if there was a car accident or I woke up late, the only response was "No excuse, sir." I didn't realize what was happening at the time, but they were training us to eliminate all excuses. Even if the reason was a "good one"—for example, if I stopped to save the life of a person who was having a heart attack—the response was still "No excuse, sir."

That's not to say that another decision should not have been made. On occasion it might have been the compassionate samurai thing to do, to save someone's life and break your commitment. Still, we didn't give in to having reasons. We simply lived with the choice.

Most people reading this haven't been trained by the military, and many aren't accustomed to the discipline I'm talking about. Realize now that you're in training for something big. Making excuses and being reasonable won't get you to the extraordinary level you desire.

Average people try hard or give it a good effort, whereas compassionate samurai do well regardless. Learn the language of a compassionate samurai: Make big commitments, keep them, and never offer reasons when you don't make things happen. Jim Stovall is a friend who frequently speaks in our Heart of the Samurai Seminar and who is a living compassionate samurai. He's the author of the best-selling book *The Ultimate Gift*, which became a major motion picture. Jim owns satellite TV stations, has won an Emmy, earned a gold medal as an Olympic weight lifter, and won Entrepreneur of the Year from the President's Committee on Equal Opportunity.

He's the only person I personally know who was also chosen as the International Humanitarian of the Year award (an honor also given to Mother Teresa). Knowing all this, it's hard to believe that Jim went blind in his early 20s. He had a very good reason to be an underachiever—at least a better one than most people have. He could have used his condition as a crutch; instead he used it to strengthen others, becoming a compassionate samurai and positively impacting hundreds of thousands of lives. You can read more about his story online at **www.theultimategift.com**. Jim is committed to making a difference.

This isn't to say that you should commit to buying out the Four Seasons hotel chain or owning a dozen McDonald's franchises (although those aren't bad ideas). Start from where you are and stretch. Maybe you can commit to being on time *all* the time for your boss or family. Perhaps you can decide to take some night classes or a weekend seminar to help better manage your time and money. Maybe you can promise yourself that you'll go out on some dates if you're widowed or have just been out of the dating game for a time.

Wherever you are, that's the place to start. Say it and begin taking steps. When you put your thoughts into words, you set wheels in motion that are moving you toward your goal. Consciously, you don't know what they are, but your subconscious is responding.

A Matter of Life and Death

"Till death do us part. For better or for worse. In sickness and in health." We've all heard these phrases in the average wedding vows many times. Do they really mean anything? Based on the divorce rates, we have to conclude they don't carry much weight with the average person. To a historical samurai, vows were a matter of life and death. Have you ever thought about being committed to anything to that extent? These warriors lived as if they were dead already; it was a fundamental way of being. This may sound morbid, but actually it's very liberating. When someone plays as if he's already dead, then he has little to lose.

Have you ever seen a fighter with nothing to lose? That person is incredibly fierce and goes full-out. When someone tries to hold on to life, however, he's hedging his bets. The average person plays not to lose, but the compassionate samurai plays with complete commitment. An ordinary individual has one foot on the gas and the other on the brakes, just in case it doesn't work out. This is the same way the average person goes into a marriage, a business, or anything else. He plays not to lose what he already has—that's one of the reasons he's average. It's been said that if a person isn't willing to die for something, he doesn't deserve to live.

- What in life would you actually die for?

- What values do you believe in so strongly that you'd give up everything rather than sacrifice those values?

- Can you think of anything right now that's actually worth dying for?

- How far would you actually go to prove your devotion to your heart's most passionate purpose?

When I contemplate these questions, it really makes me think about those who were so committed that they actually did whatever it took to fight for the cause they believed in. One of my favorite people was Martin Luther King, Jr, who led the greatest civil-rights movement ever seen in the United States. He had a beautiful wife, four lovely children, and was the pastor of the Ebenezer Baptist Church in Atlanta, Georgia. He had a lot to lose, yet he played with the commitment of a compassionate samurai.

"I won't have any money to leave behind. I won't have the fine and luxurious things of life to leave behind. But I just want to leave a committed life behind."
— Martin Luther King, Jr.

This isn't to imply that a compassionate samurai *has* to lose his life; it simply means he's willing to forfeit most of what an average person finds valuable and worthwhile. Nelson Mandela is an incredible example of a compassionate samurai. He didn't forfeit his physical life, but he did spend 27 years incarcerated in a South African prison to liberate an entire nation. Warren Buffett, one of the greatest investors of our time, has been a compassionate samurai. He has enjoyed phenomenal wealth, but he has also displayed his commitment to his values to the extent of giving almost his entire fortune of $40 billion to make a difference for humanity.

Consider how committed the terrorists were on that dreadful day—September 11, 2001—when they hijacked commercial flights and flew them into the World Trade Center and the Pentagon, killing thousands of people. They had incredible commitment. Not only did they give their lives, but there had been a failed attempt to destroy the World Trade Center in 1993, eight years before it finally came down—an eight-year commitment. The terrorists sacrificed themselves for what they believed in. Quite obviously, they don't qualify as compassionate samurai because they lacked, at a minimum, the much-needed character trait of service and contribution.

In this world, the most committed win.

∞∞

The cause that some people are willing to die for isn't always the most honorable one. It's important to realize that the good guys or the most honorable people don't always win. Morality doesn't necessarily beat immorality; good doesn't necessarily triumph over evil. *In this world, the most committed win.* That's why it's critical for the people who value an inclusive society—one that works for everyone—to continually increase their level of commitment.

There are literally billions who are currently left out. I mean the 50 percent of the people in the world who do not have clean water, the 20 percent who lack adequate shelter, and the 70 percent who are unable to read. I'm speaking of the 33 percent of the world's populace who go to bed hungry and the 3 percent who starve every year. There are many other ways of being left out as well, whether it's working at a job you hate or being alone when you want a relationship.

Compassionate samurai consider it an honor and a privilege to make a difference for others while enjoying a great life themselves. There's a compelling need for such powerful individuals today. For this cause, the team at Klemmer & Associates has dedicated their lives to building bold ethical leaders who are committed to creating a world that works for everyone, where no one is left out.

Why Some People Shy Away from Making Agreements

Why is it that average people do everything in their power *not* to make an agreement? We've already dealt with those who refuse to do so because they're more committed to looking good by not breaking a promise. It's definitely a pattern—some might even say it's an addiction they probably adopted early in life. There are some other compulsions or behaviors that average people choose that prevent them from making better agreements and achieving extraordinary results. Some of those low-level exchanges include:

- Looking good
- Being comfortable
- Being right
- Being accepted

Some people are committed to looking good, so they don't make agreements that they might not be able to follow through on. Others are committed to just being comfortable. They refuse to push higher or go any farther than where they are right now. Do you know anyone whose main goal in life is to just be comfortable? Many times, they'll say things like "Why should I attend a self-improvement seminar? I'm fine." And maybe they are. However, they're missing out on how much more they could be and could do for themselves and for others. They let their *good* stand in the way of their *spectacular.*

In fact, these people often resent those who challenge and push them to the next level. If in *being* more, you can inevitably *do* more for others, then your unwillingness to grow is really taking away from those around you. It's a self-centered, selfish attitude. Other people are so committed to being right that they can't make any agreements that might put them in a position of perhaps being wrong. They want nothing more in life than just to be right. Klemmer & Associates has consulted with some companies where average managers were more committed to being right about the reasons that things couldn't change than they were to making modifications for a better, more lucrative working environment.

Have you ever been in an argument with a loved one and accused the other person of being wrong about something as trivial as how long ago an event occurred? An argument that small can jeopardize your relationship. Then, because you wanted to be right, you didn't talk to your loved one for two days—perhaps you weren't intimate for more than a week. I've been there. Divorce often happens because people are more committed to being right than to the relationship working. A compassionate samurai has a sense of priorities and doesn't make an issue of trivialities when it isn't necessary.

Although there's nothing intrinsically wrong with being right, it forces a situation in which someone has to be wrong. In some cases, more than one person is correct. For example, imagine a book with a blue front cover and a red back cover. A person looking at it from the front would say the book is blue, but a person looking at it from behind would say it's red. Could they get into an argument about who's right? Certainly. Compassionate samurai make an agreement with themselves to live outside this box wherever possible.

Other individuals shun making agreements in order to be accepted. Average people in the workplace won't agree to large goals because they're afraid of losing the acceptance of those who don't want to work hard; many schoolchildren don't make commitments to excel because they want to fit in with their classmates. The bottom line is that a compassionate samurai never runs away from agreements. Rather, he runs toward them, knowing that they're the basis of life and productivity.

The Fear of Making Agreements

Much of people's hesitation in making commitments revolves around fear. They're afraid that they aren't capable of meeting their pledge, or they believe that it restrains them from being able to do what they want to do. There's also an interesting perception that obligation constrains choice. It's true that you do lose the option of doing what you want to do in the moment, but there's so much more to gain when you keep your word. At the risk of being stereotypical, many men are afraid of committing to marriage for this same reason. They always wonder, *What if a better option comes along?*

My mentor taught me that "rules create liberty." Look at rules for the moment as agreements. If there were no standards for driving, you and everyone else could do as you pleased. You could stop or go at a green light, and the oncoming traffic could do the same. What if there were no agreement about which side of the road to drive on? If there were no speed limit, you could go 2 miles per hour, and perhaps the guy behind you could go 100 miles per hour. Given that scenario, would you have more freedom or less? The answer is less, particularly since you might wind up dead. Rules create liberty.

Compassionate samurai are clear about the agreements when they hire someone in business. They're also very clear about the rules of marriage when they propose. Most people assume that everyone is going by their roles even when they haven't made it clear what those are. That's dangerous! Imagine if you and I played a game of football, but I played according to the American rules, and you played by the European ones (what Americans know as soccer). There would not be liberty in the game. There would be chaos and confusion; it would be a total mess. Learn to make agreements to give yourself and others more liberty.

Overcommitment

People who are overcommitted are invested in being liked and viewed as nice guys. For the most part, they're just afraid of rejection. I've seen people do this frequently in their professional lives. They'll sign on to do a job that they don't have the time or the proper staff to handle because they're afraid they'll lose revenue by not accepting the job. Yet, the scenario will work out quite differently than they imagine. They'll please their customer in the short term, but not in the long term.

There's an old adage in business that you make money by the jobs you turn down. This has several different meanings. For example, if you accept a job just to be a nice guy or because you're afraid of losing opportunities, you'll end up breaking agreements that involve meeting deadlines, and it will cost you more in referrals.

Abundance is another trait that a compassionate samurai operates from; it's covered later in the book. With an abundance mind-set, you can say no. You're already paying a price for overcommitting, which is usually larger than what's obvious at first. A compassionate samurai pays the short-term price of being uncomfortable and saying no in order to reap the long-term enjoyment of being a man of his word.

Everyone Is Committed Whether They Know It or Not

If you've been following this discussion, you're beginning to realize that everyone is committed. It's just that average people aren't devoted to what they think they are. That's why the familiar statement "I have a problem with commitment" is ridiculous. You may be determined to not make agreements, to not trust others, or to play small, but you're still very much committed. A compassionate samurai is dedicated to results and to the ten character traits covered in this book. Average people struggle with conflicting commitments between their conscious and subconscious mind.

A compassionate samurai has clarity and integrity because his conscious and subconscious mind are committed to the same thing. Oftentimes we have a strategy in life that works for us, but then it prevents us from becoming even more successful—it actually becomes a weakness. This has been referred to as a competing commitment. Here are some questions you can use to determine what your competing commitment is:

1. What do I consistently do to present myself as valuable and useful in the eyes of others?

2. What am I really good at? What do I consider a "main strength" that I keep reverting back to?

3. How do I appear to others in order to gauge my personal worth?

4. If I'm really successful, what do I fear may change in my relationships with my friends and family?

5. What have I always been told I was good at?

6. What act of pretension do I go to work with that keeps me from fully connecting with others?

I created my value through my work ethic and self-confidence, which helped me academically. I wasn't the smartest kid in high school or at West Point. However, I worked harder than many of my peers to get into the academy, and I was frequently on the dean's list once I got there. It also helped in sports. I was small in high school—about 5'7" and around 165 pounds. Again my hustle, confidence, and work ethic enabled me to play varsity football. I was even awarded Most Valuable Defensive Player at my senior Thanksgiving Day game.

I wasn't talented, but my dedication to my work ethic as an entrepreneur helped build Klemmer & Associates into a successful company that earns $10 million annually. However, for us to grow to $100 million a year, I need to change. As of the printing of this book, we haven't reached that goal, but it's our commitment. I wrote it down here to hold our staff and myself accountable. I discovered that my strength had become a weakness. Working harder than most of the employees and bursting with so much self-confidence actually prevented me from fully connecting with many of my co-workers and thus capturing their full participation and potential.

They occasionally had to see me filled with doubt, or vulnerable at times. They had to know that I didn't have all the answers or they wouldn't feel needed. So my competing commitment became my need to establish worth by hard work and total confidence to my determination to grow the company. *Everyone* has competing commitments. Compassionate samurai are clear about their devotion to their principles and that's always superior to any competing obligations.

For more on this idea, you may want to explore *Theory of Constraints* by Eliyahu Goldratt or *How the Way We Talk Can Change the Way We Work* by Robert Kegan and Lisa Laskow Lahey. For example, when artisans craft real samurai swords (not replicas), they heat, fold, and beat two types of steel 80,000 times. This process gives the weapons their incredible strength and sharpness. The practice of making big agreements and keeping them is just that—a practice. After thousands of rehearsals, you can learn and become this first trait of a compassionate samurai.

1. What is the biggest agreement you've made and kept?

2. What new and bigger agreement can you make and keep?

"Knock down seven times. Get up eight."
— Samurai saying

Compassionate samurai choose to.

Average people have to.

Chapter Two

PERSONAL RESPONSIBILITY

*"A man can fail many times, but he isn't a failure
until he begins to blame someone else."*
— Unknown

There's one viewpoint that most people hate to accept, and it is that *everything you have, don't have, and ever will have in life is because of the choices you make.* Yet that's exactly the attitude compassionate samurai take, even if they don't think it's true. They believe that where they are is directly connected to the choices they make. Average people take the stance of a victim—that is, that life happens to them.

I'm reminded of an old story about a construction worker who carries his lunch to work in a black metal can. He opens the can and starts to complain about the peanut butter-and-jelly sandwich he has for lunch. This scene repeats itself every afternoon. Day after day he complains about his peanut butter-and-jelly sandwich for lunch. By the end of the week, his co-workers are pretty tired of his whining, and one asks, "Why don't you just tell your wife to make you a roast beef or tuna sandwich for lunch?"

He replies, "Wife? I don't have a wife. I made this sandwich myself." That may sound a bit ridiculous, but it illustrates the point that the average person makes his or her "sandwich of life" and then complains about it. So let's build our case for the viewpoint that everything you have, don't have, and ever will have is because of the choices you make. Taking this position will cause you to play life as a compassionate samurai. No one does anything just because; there has to be something in it for you.

Here are the benefits of playing life by the rule that everything I am is because of me:

1. It improves your experience and what you're feeling, even if your circumstances don't change.

2. It gives you the potential for different outcomes.

3. It puts you back in the driver's seat. You're in control.

It's Your Choice

Every moment is a choice, and every choice has consequences—both costs and benefits. That's how we start our Klemmer & Associates Teen Leadership seminars. The kids will argue at first. They'll say something like "No, I have to go to school." Our facilitator will reply, "No, you don't." The back and forth of "Yes, I do" and "No, you don't" is amusing. But finally, one of the teenagers will say something along these lines: "If I don't go to school, they'll put me in a juvenile-detention facility." The facilitator will agree, saying, "That's true, and that's called a consequence. You're choosing to go to school instead of going to a juvenile-detention center." Thus, the teenager begins to understand that every moment he or she has a choice, and that every decision has consequences.

Just realizing that each moment is a choice changes our experience. Try saying "I have to" about something in your life, such as " I have to go to work." What do you feel? Most likely you may experience low energy, frustration, maybe even depression. Now try saying, "I choose to go to work." What do you feel now? You probably feel more energetic and upbeat.

It's the same activity, but picking a different viewpoint changes your experience. This is the primary benefit in selecting the power of choice instead of being a victim, because you create experiences for yourself. Being personally responsible means taking the attitude that you're the cause of your experience because of the choices you decide to make. You, too, will become a compassionate samurai when you choose to see that you're personally responsible for everything in your life.

You're responsible for the way the relationships
in your life are working right now.

Let's go into a bit of detail here. The amount of money that you earn each week, month, or year is directly connected to your choices, and you're personally responsible for your income. Yet I've heard people complain over and over again about their jobs, but they stay there for years—even until retirement. That's *Joe Average Man* or *Mary Ann Mediocre*. It seems a bit insane, yet people do it every day. The quality or lack thereof in your marriage, your relationship with your children, your relationship with your parents or in-laws, and the very state of being single or married are all a direct result of the choices you've made.

You're responsible for how the relationships in your life are working right now. People complain about someone for years and still pretend they didn't make that sandwich themselves. They ignore the fact that they chose to date the person or not to exercise due diligence before entering a permanent commitment. They disregard the contribution that their attitude or lack of forgiveness makes to their partner's actions. Why does anyone stay in a dead-end position? First of all, the average person doesn't believe that he has a choice.

People tend to believe that they have to take whatever life gives them. If you believe that you're worth more than you're being paid and you can justify your reasoning, then ask for a raise. However, many folks just complain and never take action. If you ask for an increase and are turned down, it doesn't mean that you aren't worth the amount of money you're requesting. It only means that your employer doesn't see your value the way you do. The simple solution is to find a company that recognizes your worth or start your own business.

Many people are so afraid of not finding another job that they choose security over opportunity and pretend they don't have a choice. If you continue to stay where you aren't paid well or are underappreciated, then it's your choice. In the final analysis, you're responsible for your economic future. Now you're thinking, *This guy really doesn't know my wife,* or *Brian has no idea how much of a jerk my boss actually is.* Listen, I'm trying to tell you that those things really don't matter.

It's not about what these people do or don't do. Rather, it's all about how you *respond* to what they do and whether you're willing to continue your life under these conditions. That's totally up to you. It's like a ship setting sail: It really doesn't matter which way the wind blows or what direction the current is moving. What matters is how the sails or rudder are responding.

I know you're probably thinking about all of the tragic things that have occurred in your life and how they really weren't fair. They happened to you, and you didn't deserve it. Okay, once you finish venting, keep reading. It's clear that you've had quite a few problems. What compassionate samurai hasn't? There isn't a warrior of any sort who couldn't share a list of troubles with you. The longer you live, the longer your personal list will become. From the moment you're born, you have challenges: how you're going to be fed, how your diapers are going to be changed, who's going to play with you, and who's going to burp you after you've eaten. As you get older, you deal with different problems. You start school and encounter bullies; name-calling becomes a real issue because no one likes to be picked on.

Then you begin your teenage years and go through puberty. Your hormones kick in, and you have no idea what's going on with your body. Girls and guys you once thought you hated are suddenly beautiful, desirable angels. Being cool and looking good is now a major concern because you have to fit in; peer pressure rears its ugly head. Then you're off to college, and you have to study harder than you ever have before. You think that your professor is absolutely insane giving you 15 books— each three inches thick—to read for the semester. Exams are coming, and that's a problem because you haven't been studying. You persevere, and finally you graduate. You've gotten your diploma, and you're really proud. But after three months of trying to find a job, you're pretty discouraged. You have a degree but no job. That's a major problem because your student loans are coming due in another couple of months.

You get a job. Now your problems are over, right? Think again. You've got to find the right partner for the rest of your life. That can be very difficult in a big world that offers so many choices. You discover the person of your dreams . . . and your dream becomes a nightmare. Now you have to recast your desires. And don't forget about the kids you have to raise and pay for, including college and weddings. Then they're out of the house, and you're ready to start living. . . .

You are never without the ability to choose in life.

∞∞

But you're older and you have arthritis, so you begin subscribing to AARP to find out how mature adults deal with these issues. And then you die. Your troubles are over! Or are they? They may really just be starting.

I just took you on a mock journey through your life to show you that problems are always going to exist on every level. The only time they'll disappear is when you die. Depending on your religious convictions, however, even after you leave this world you may still have some issues about where you'll wind up.

Problems aren't a bad thing. They help us mature into phenomenal people and also activate our power to choose. *We are never without the ability to choose in life.* I know that bad things happen to good people, but how we decide to respond to those events makes all the difference in the world. Even in an extreme situation such as abuse, there's still choice. Please don't think that I'm being insensitive. I'm very empathetic toward anyone who has been in an abusive relationship, and I condemn all forms of abuse. The truth remains, though, that even in such a situation we have options. They aren't easy. Each one carries heavy potential consequences, but there are still choices to be made in selecting the person and in how we respond.

In A.D. 68, the Maccabees, a Jewish family, took on the Roman Empire. Put aside your opinion about whether you think it was right or wrong, a good decision or a bad one. It was a choice, and there were benefits and costs. The Maccabees held out for approximately three years in the palace King Herod had built at Masada. I've actually visited the place, and it's spectacular. Imagine a thumb rising 1,200 feet out of the desert. At the top, there's a fort—that's Masada. It took the Romans three years to build a hill to the top of the cliff, and it was obvious they were going to capture the fort.

So the Maccabees met and explored their choices. Rather than allow their children to become slaves and their wives to be abused, they decided to rob the Romans of the satisfaction of determining how they were going to die. One thousand people willfully committed suicide. Again, put aside how you feel about their decision. This is merely an extreme example to illustrate that we always have choices. Again, I'm not suggesting killing yourself as a solution to untenable circumstances. This story simply shows a decision with different benefits and prices.

As you can see from the Maccabees and Masada, even when you can't see an alternative, it doesn't mean that you don't have one. The ability to discover choices gives you an experience that's different from not seeing any, even if all the options are bad and have limited benefits.

Have you ever heard of Viktor Frankl? He was an Austrian neurologist and psychiatrist who survived the Holocaust. He witnessed nearly every possible atrocity toward humans, and yet he survived. Both his parents died in the concentration camps, and even his wife was murdered. Frankl watched people starve to death, scurrying to find a morsel of bread, doing anything they could to live. He witnessed the torture of his fellow inmates and saw people brutally killed. The only relative who survived was his sister, and she emigrated to Australia. Most people would have given up after enduring such atrocities, but Frankl said that he chose to discover the meaning in various forms of existence, even the most sordid ones.

It was to that end that he wrote his famous work *Man's Search for Meaning,* which chronicles his life in the concentration camps and how he used the power of his mind and redirected his focus to survive. Under the most reprehensible conditions, Frankl still maintained that choice was the driving factor that kept him alive. As set out in the book, he believes that the power of choice can also keep others alive even in the most trying times:

> We who lived in concentration camps can remember the men who walked through the huts comforting others, giving away their last piece of bread. They may have been few in number, but they offer sufficient proof that everything can be taken from a man but one thing: the last of the human freedoms—to choose one's attitude in any given set of circumstances, to choose one's own way.

The quality of your life—or its lack of quality—is your choice. And this is all about taking personal responsibility for what you do. It's also about how you respond to other people's actions toward you.

Options and Liberty

Here's a novel thought: *All people have freedom.* What about those who live under a dictator? They, too, have freedom. Why? Because it's the ability to choose, and all human beings have that, as Viktor Frankl has so eloquently described, even in unimaginable circumstances. However, the consequences of their choices are far different from average circumstances. And even though all people have freedom, very few enjoy liberty.

Liberty is the ability to do what you want to do when you want to do it, to go where you want to go when you want to go there. Most important, it's the ability to be what you want to be when you want to be it.

Compassionate samurai search for choices, solutions, and meaning in life, rather than waiting for them to appear. They try to increase the liberty that they and others enjoy. They don't shrink from tough choices simply because they don't like the perceived outcomes.

I believe that of all the gifts God grants us, the most powerful is *choice*. It's also a very useful tool if used skillfully. It has a power that gives us the potential winner's edge all of the time. It's the ability to create liberty. That might sound like an unrealistic philosophy, but it isn't. What you pick now determines what you enjoy tomorrow. What you decide not to choose also determines what you'll never have in this lifetime.

So at the end of the day—or even at the end of your life—you can be an average person and blame others for what did or didn't happen for you. Or you can be a compassionate samurai and enjoy yourself even amid dire circumstances and create a life of liberty for yourself and others.

If liberty is so great, why aren't there more compassionate samurai experiencing it? The answer is because there's a cost for everything. There's no free lunch. Every benefit has a corresponding cost or something you must give up. There's a price to acknowledging that you have choices (as there are different consequences for pretending that you don't). There are costs for making the compassionate samurai choice, as well as for taking the easier way out. At West Point, we were taught always to choose the harder right rather than the easier wrong. They were teaching us to be compassionate samurai. Some might argue about the compassionate part, but we'll save that for another discussion.

If we wimp out and don't make the
right choices, we lose our liberty.

Frankl once recommended the Statue of Liberty on the East Coast be complemented by a "Statue of Responsibility" on the West Coast. Perhaps he was saying that our liberty requires us to make good decisions. If we wimp out and don't make the right choices, we lose our liberty. When we do this, we choose obvious short-term benefits with not-so-obvious long-term costs over obvious short-term costs that have not-so-obvious long-term benefits. The very nature of a compassionate samurai is to pick the latter.

I'm concerned with what I see in American society; in fact, that was the impetus for writing this book. Listen to average people complain about how their children won't benefit from the Social Security program, yet they're unwilling to change their lifestyle in any way. Look at how average people enjoy the benefits of their current status, but they shrink from considering the future environmental impact of their excesses on their grandchildren—even to the point of being "confused" about whether global warming and other such issues are real.

Consider those who made huge amounts of money in the Enron, Tyco, and even Arthur Andersen scandals, with no concern for the thousands who lost their retirement savings as a result—let alone the damages the economy suffered or the cynicism about business that was generated. This isn't really a new thing. Such behavior has occurred throughout history in nations and families who received abundance rather than earning it. A different, higher value is established when something is earned. When life is painful enough, moving forward becomes a more obvious and easier choice to make for the average individual.

For a compassionate samurai, the immediate dis-comfort is irrelevant if it's outweighed by long-term benefits. Samurai endured great physical pain, particularly when wounded in battle. Despite this, the agony of violating the warrior codes was far worse. At the founding of our country, 56 brave souls put their signatures on the Declaration of Independence. By signing that document, they knew that they were putting their families, fortunes, and lives in jeopardy for the opportunity to pursue liberty for themselves and others. They were, without a doubt, compassionate samurai. Because of their act of courage, we now enjoy liberty. You may wonder if they paid a price. The answer is absolutely yes!

- Five signers were captured by the British as traitors and tortured before they died.

- Twelve had their homes ransacked and burned.

- Two lost their sons serving in the Army; another had two sons captured.

- Nine fought and died from the wounds or hardships of the Revolutionary War.

That's just the short list of the high price that those men paid. Being a compassionate samurai isn't a free ride through life with all benefits. There are major costs involved. We've received liberty, but now we must re-create its value or our heirs will lose it. Remember, excitement builds momentum, but only character lasts.

> *"The choice is no longer between violence and nonviolence; it is either nonviolence or nonexistence."*
> — Martin Luther King, Jr., "The American Dream" speech, Lincoln University, Oxford, Pennsylvania, June 6, 1961

Liberty is more precious than gold and silver and requires more discipline to obtain and maintain. In his book *The Burden of Freedom,* Dr. Myles Munroe refers to irresponsibility as freedom's greatest enemy. He is using the word *freedom* in the same way I'm using *liberty.* He says, "You are where you are because you have subconsciously chosen to be." That means many of our choices are made by our sub-conscious. Of irresponsibility Munroe writes:

> The word irresponsibility also carries with it the meaning of "lacking conscience" or "unable or unwilling to respond to conscience." It is mankind's conscience that allows us to distinguish between right and wrong. When a lifestyle of irresponsibility is allowed to increase, the voice of conscience is progressively silenced. Some people are doing unbelievable things, yet they have no

sense of guilt or remorse after they've finished. People are shooting each other. Husbands are beating their wives. Fathers sleep with their daughters, wake up, shower, eat breakfast and go off to work as if nothing happened. Conscience has died throughout much of the world's society because we have inherited a spirit of irresponsibility.

If what Munroe is saying is true—and I believe that it is—then we can directly correlate liberty to responsibility and bondage to irresponsibility. Isn't it true that many of the inmates of our prisons acted irresponsibly, which is why they've lost their liberty? If you drive down the street at 100 miles an hour in a school zone, for example, you will lose your liberty to drive. Or, as an attorney, if you participate in fraudulent actions and are disbarred, then you lose your privilege to practice law.

Liberty is removed, sometimes permanently, as a consequence of irresponsible behavior. It's lost when average people fail to act responsibly. If this is true, then the only way to maintain liberty in every area of our lives is to become personally accountable for our own actions. That means that you and I must become true compassionate samurai. It's important to see that not all the choices, benefits, and costs are grandiose. People make choices every day. The challenge comes in two sets of circumstances:

1. When there are immediate benefits to the poor choice and the long-term costs are hidden

2. When there are obvious costs to the right choice and the long-term benefits are hidden

In our Klemmer & Associates Leadership Seminars, we often help our participants identify areas in which they think there are no choices and then we illuminate the alternatives they do have. This can be a very difficult process because they must release all the benefits they receive from pretending that they don't have any options or from assuming the role of a victim. Let's look at some of the benefits of being a victim:

1. It exempts you from having to take action.

2. People feel sorry for you and have pity parties for you—and that makes you feel good, wanted, accepted, and loved.

3. You never have to make tough decisions.

4. You don't feel obligated to do anything great in life; "the thing" that happened is responsible for the way you are.

5. For the rest of your life, you can comfortably believe that your failures are directly connected to what someone else did to you, and you can blame them.

People love to be victims because of these benefits. When they live this way, they never have to feel personally responsible for anything that happens to them. Consider Oprah Winfrey, who at an early age was molested by family members more than once. She could have very easily chosen to follow the path of countless others who experienced the same trauma.

Instead she used the thing that could have crippled her to advance her cause in life—helping people. Do you think that because she chose not to allow the rape to stop her that she's trivializing it? Some people do. They believe that if she doesn't air her pain to the world, she's somehow allowing the rapist to escape punishment. But this isn't about justice; it's about who lives life to the fullest. It's already pretty obvious that a rapist isn't living life to his optimal capacity; if he were, he wouldn't have to commit such a crime.

Today, as the owner of a television network, Oprah is in a far better position to expose every child molester in America. If she'd allowed herself to become a victim, she would have limited her influence and power to help millions achieve their freedom. Choosing not to be a victim isn't only about you; it's also about those you're assigned to help set free. Still, some people would much rather be victims because it brings immediate benefits.

Dr. Ben Carson, a noted neurosurgeon, became the director of the pediatric neurosurgery department at the Johns Hopkins Hospital when he was only 33 years old. He's among the most skilled in his field in the world. Dr. Carson became famous for his ability to surgically separate conjoined twins, a feat that many of his peers haven't been able to do. But his life didn't start off with great success.

He was born in Detroit to a single mother. She married at the age of 13, but when Carson was 8 years old, his parents divorced. His mother worked three and four jobs to try to provide a decent living for her sons. Although she didn't even get past the third grade, she wanted Ben and his older brother, Curtis, to have a better education than she'd had. Ben was taunted by his schoolmates, who often called him "Dummy" when he couldn't answer questions in class. His response to their name-calling was uncontrollable anger. As a teenager, Ben almost killed another boy because he couldn't control his rage. That was a life-defining moment.

Instead of becoming a statistic, he chose to educate himself beyond the slurs that were thrown at him. Ben astonished his classmates over and over again with his unusual mastery of scientific knowledge. Eventually, he graduated from Yale University with a degree in psychology and received his medical degree from the University of Michigan. Dr. Carson could have easily chosen to become a victim and reaped the benefits of doing so. Fortunately, he realized the same thing that true warriors realize: There's no enduring, long-lasting, life-improving benefit to being a victim. That choice keeps you right where you are.

I'm Not Your Problem

No one in life is your problem. You may say, "My mother wasn't there for me," or "My dad talked to me like I was crap." That may be, but they aren't your problem. Your boss, your professor, your up-line recruiter, your drill sergeant, not even your children are your problem. These are people, not problems. The only difficulties there are in life are the ones that you appoint. Another way of looking at it is that problems only exist because you haven't solved them yet.

I've heard mothers blame the fact that they had children at an early age for why they couldn't go to college or pursue a career. They made their kids their problem, when in fact, the family was an excuse for them not to move forward. It's interesting to see how people choose to make certain things an issue while others use the same thing to their advantage.

Ben Carson's mother, Sonya, used the fact that she had two children and no help to motivate her to provide the best life and example for her sons that she could. She didn't have an education, but she made sure that her children would. Sonya asked Ben and his brother to write book reviews, two each week, and turn them in to her for review. After that, they were allowed to go outside and play with the other kids. She couldn't read very well, and she couldn't really even assess whether the reports were correct. But none of that mattered. She knew that her kids weren't her problem. Carson's father (who'd walked out on the family when Carson was eight) wasn't her problem or the boys'. They could have easily made that man their excuse. But what good would that have done? Not much. Remember, *no one* is your problem. You take responsibility for everything. You're in control. You alone are in the driver's seat—no one else.

This Isn't a Blame Game

Of all games, the blame game has to be the biggest waste of time because nothing changes. To assign fault yourself or others is an absolute waste of time in terms of actually solving the problem. For the moment, you may feel better, but nothing really changes.

Years ago, in one of his stand-up comedy acts, Bill Cosby joked about kids who grow up as only children and the dilemma they face because they don't have siblings to blame for their mistakes. In some ways, he was saying that having brothers and sisters gives rise to blaming. That may be true, but it's not always healthy. I know from raising my children that blaming siblings weakens a child's ability to be truly accountable for his or her actions. And surprisingly, it starts early in life. For example, someone will spill milk on the floor. The parent asks, "Who did it?" And the child instinctively points at someone else, knowing that she has to satisfy her parent, even if the person she's pointing at happens to be the wrong person. She's solving the problem of being pressured by giving an incorrect answer. Another way to resolve the stress is by understanding that being responsible and being blamed have nothing to do with each other. Being personally responsible acknowledges the choices we've made, and that's very different than blame.

A compassionate samurai understands that and consequently has no interest or time for blame. Imagine if I had an argument with my wife. I made more than 1,000 conscious choices that helped set the stage for the argument: I chose to marry her, to bring up a certain topic when she was tired and had other things on her mind, and to get angry at her response. Does any of that mean I'm at fault for the fight? No! A compassionate samurai separates fault and blame from personal responsibility and thus is willing to assume the responsibility for everything.

A closely related reason for not operating from a place of responsibility is held by many Christians. I see this because I'm a born-again Christian. Their paradigm of either/or (which we'll address more fully in the chapter on abundance) encompasses the idea that either I am responsible or God is. That "box" means that if I'm going to be responsible, I must deny that God is all-powerful. This reasoning sounds humanistic, so a fundamentalist believer would reject it. Or if I let God be all-powerful, then I'm the victim because it's "God's will."

Unfortunately, this is where many Christians are. They blame the devil or God, so they don't have to be responsible. In my humble opinion, this is hogwash. God is all-powerful, and we are responsible. It's not either/or; it's both. It's exactly what we've been discussing. We always have choices, but that has nothing to do with who's at fault, which really doesn't matter.

∞∞

*Compassionate samurai give
without thought of personal gain.*

*Average people give when there's something
in it for them, and it doesn't cost too much.*

Chapter Three

CONTRIBUTION

"We make a living by what we get.
We make a life by what we give."
— Winston Churchill

What is the bigger picture in life? For the compassionate samurai, looking at the bigger picture always leads to the question *How can I serve this person, organization, or country?* In fact, the true meaning of the word *samurai* is "to serve." The average person always asks, *What's in it for me?* The average businessperson leads an ordinary life; an extraordinary one makes a great profit and always wins in the marketplace. But compassionate samurai businesspeople, in addition to being highly successful, choose to make a great contribution to their community, their society, the people who work with and for them, and their customers.

Compassionate samurai also give to those they'll never see in this lifetime by leaving a positive legacy. They not only make contributions; they *are* living gifts. These individuals realize that whatever they have isn't solely for their own use; it's also for the benefit of others. This includes their finances, time, talents, even life itself. No matter where they are, compassionate samurai are always looking for ways to contribute.

Sometimes there's something in it for them and sometimes not. At some points they have lots to give and at others they don't. Regardless of their personal circumstances, they live a life of giving. In 1570, during the war for the unification of Japan, the battle of Anegawa took place. The armies of Asakura Yoshikage and Tokugawa Ieyasu, two great daimyos or warlords, were engaged in battle when Asakura's army became surrounded. To give Asakura an opportunity to retreat and reorganize, one of his grand champions, Makara Jurozaemon, offered a challenge.

A champion from Tokugawa's army accepted his challenge. Makara won the fight, and then another of Tokugawa's champions fought him. This continued until eventually Makara was beaten and beheaded. His son stayed beside him during these battles while the rest of Asakura's army retreated. The son was beheaded as well. Makara gave his life to save the army, and his son gave himself to support his father. Not only did they save the army, but also they gained honor and a legacy that exists to this day, more than 400 years later.

Compassionate samurai are willing to give their lives for a great cause or for their principles. An average person values his existence above all else; he wants to survive at all costs. This isn't to say that compassionate samurai are martyrs who always give until they have nothing left. Some people do adopt this mind-set. They give their time to their children, job, and community, but they never spend time on themselves. This results in burnout, and then there's nothing left for anyone. Some folks donate money to their churches and other causes but never invest anything for themselves. As a result, they generally don't have large amounts for any cause. They're willing to give everything if the circumstance requires it, but martyrs neglect themselves under the cloak of nobility.

Giving to Yourself

In terms of giving, what's the difference between a martyr and a compassionate samurai? The difference is what is at stake. Compassionate samurai take care of themselves as they lead a service lifestyle. Giving to themselves is okay; they don't feel guilty receiving. Martyrs, on the other hand, often feel guilty when they gain something for their own purposes, thinking that it may violate their objective. Being generous with yourself increases your capacity to help others. In fact, it's part of the giving lifestyle. Giving to yourself is not acceptable, however, if it's done at the expense or to the exclusion of others.

If you give all your money away, you live like a pauper and have no reserves to sustain yourself or others in challenging times. If you don't spend time on yourself to take care of your body, you won't have a life to give. Don't mistake this for selfishness; it's appropriate self-worth that says, "I am worthy, as are others." Compassionate samurai give continually, and that includes themselves. They appreciate the value and blessing of life.

Six Benefits of Giving

Why give at all? To adopt the lifestyle of a compassionate samurai means contributing whether it's comfortable or difficult to do so, whether you want to or not, and whether there's anything in it for you or not. This can be difficult. So let's build a case that will substantiate why you should give, and then you'll be far more willing to rise to the challenge. There are six primary benefits:

1. It feels good.
2. You give to get.
3. It builds loyalty.
4. It increases your power.
5. Giving without recognition increases your power.
6. It increases your spirituality.

The first benefit of giving is that it just plain feels good—and there's nothing wrong with feeling good. It may not always feel great, but usually it does. It's actually cheaper than drugs—and it's not illegal. Have you ever seen a Girl Scout selling cookies? Try giving her $100 and buying a carton. You'll smile all day long! A technique I learned from someone I consider a compassionate samurai, Bob Harrison (**www.increase.org**), is to carry an extra $100 bill in my wallet at all times. Whenever I feel the call, I give the cash to someone. The joy of living is in giving.

The second benefit of giving is that you get. It's a law—not a law of society, but one like gravity. It's impossible not to gain when you give. A farmer understands this;

he or she sows seed in the earth and expects a harvest. Companies deliver to customers and obtain their business. Nordstrom is famous for its service: Sales staff will take you all over their store, making sure you get exactly what you want and giving you first-class treatment. Starbucks has earned a reputation for exceptional service as well. Partners (employees) are taught to memorize a regular customer's name and the drink he or she prefers.

Some people are confused by the idea of giving. They expect the recipient to always return something to them. That's not always the case. The reward could come from another person or place. The average individual who feels exploited by a company often slacks off, thinking, *I don't get paid to handle this grief.* A compassionate samurai would keep contributing to the company, knowing that this opens up the universe to some other organization that will offer her a better job with higher pay. People give to politicians, knowing that they'll most likely garner favor. (This is trading rather than giving. You offer a resource and expect something from that person in return.)

The third benefit received from giving is loyalty. If, for example, as a supervisor, you give your subordinates opportunity, protection, mentoring, and so on, they'll most likely be very loyal to you. When you assist someone, that person will instinctively believe that he owes you something, and that something is usually loyalty.

The fourth benefit received from giving is power. You'll especially gain this if you give anonymously. If people know that you were the donor, then you gain recognition. For an interesting review of this concept, read *The Magnificent Obsession* by Lloyd C. Douglas, or watch the movie starring Rock Hudson and Jane Wyman.

*Men or women demonstrate their power not by how much
they accumulate but by how much they give.*

When you give without receiving any recognition, something supernatural occurs—you gain power or influence that's inexplicable. Men or women demonstrate their power not by how much they accumulate, but by how much they give. Contribution is actually self-serving, but it's almost counterintuitive. Most of us grow up thinking that we live in a dog-eat-dog world and that if we don't take care of ourselves, no one else will. That concept is a myopic short-term philosophy. The more I look out for "number one," the more everyone around me does the same, and then I find myself living in a competitive world instead of a cooperative world that builds additional possibilities.

The sixth benefit is spirituality. Look at anyone of almost any faith whom you consider spiritual. They're givers. This behavior rejects the spirit of this world (mammon) and reaffirms God's spirit. This is why tithing is such a great practice. On a repeated emotional level as you give away the first tenth of everything you earn, you're making a statement that money doesn't control you.

If you give to the place where you receive your spiritual nourishment, you're affirming how important it actually is to you. Average people are gripped by the fear of scarcity. Since they believe that they're the source of things, they're afraid that giving will decrease what they have. Even if you don't accept this spiritual principle, it can still increase your prosperity. These benefits are all gained by anyone who gives.

Here is a key distinction between average individuals and the compassionate samurai: Average people aren't big givers. When they do contribute, their primary motive is one of the six benefits mentioned earlier. Compassionate samurai think *service before self.* They believe it's a good thing to give, and it's greater when the motive is selfless. Compassionate samurai frequently bless others without any thought of return.

There's nothing wrong with giving and expecting something back. That's simply the law of sowing and reaping at work. A far greater concept is to give without the thought of where your harvest will come from. It's somewhat like the concept of *agape* love. God blesses us all unconditionally, whether or not we give back to Him. The challenge here is to think about contribution on a totally new level. It's easy to do more for the customer who gives the most to you. After all, one hand washes the other, right? The average person tends to have a "what's in it for me" mind-set. He won't give unless there is something coming back.

Compassionate samurai know that they'll get something back, but that's not why they give. They consider it an honor and a privilege to serve their fellow beings. It's their reason for existence. They recognize the connectedness of all human beings and are committed to making a difference for others. They realize that their body isn't who they are; it doesn't define them. Consequently, they're interested in a bigger picture that involves all of humanity.

Give Them What They Want, Not What You Want to Give Them

When average people think about giving to others, a screen goes up and hides all of the things that they don't really want to relinquish, enabling them to let go of whatever they'd like to and have plenty left. What's best to give in our eyes isn't always best in the eyes of the recipient. Giving means donating what's wanted and needed by others, not what we want. It's just human nature to tend to go with what we think folks need, rather than what they're crying out for.

In some ways, this can be an arrogant exercise. Our ego tells us pretty regularly that we always know what someone else needs. One of the most basic ways to find out what a person, community, or church could use is to ask! Many times, it's that simple. In our seminars, I've heard thousands of husbands talk about working hard and providing a beautiful house, clothes, and great lifestyle for their families. When you listen to their wives, however, you discover that they'd gladly take a smaller house or fewer vacations if they could have their husbands at a few more of the children's sports games or music recitals.

Many wives take great care of their children and have spotless homes, yet their husbands would rather have an unkempt living room and a few more take-out meals if their wives had more energy to be intimate at the end of the day. I'm not attempting to stereotype roles here. The point is that we often give others what we think they need without ever asking what they really want.

Sometimes at work we spend a lot of time doing what we like, but it's not adding value to the company. All of our hard work really isn't of service, because it's not what is wanted. Have you ever just simply asked your boss what she'd like you to handle? How long has it been since you've asked your spouse or child what you can do for them? One time, my son Kelly and I were on a father-son vacation in Hawaii, where I'd planned fishing trips and all kinds of activities. Then I stopped myself and practiced the art of a compassionate samurai by simply asking him what he thought would be fun.

Kelly replied that what he really wanted to do was watch the action movies his mother wasn't fond of him seeing. I decided that for one day on vacation it would be fine, and for the next nine hours, we watched back-to-back action movies. We ordered pizza and didn't even leave the room. To this day, it's one of his favorite memories of the two of us. He wanted time with me in a certain way. He didn't want my advice or what I thought would be fun. Not only did I get a great time with him, but afterward he listened to me in a different way.

Sometimes people may ask you to do something you don't like or you find uncomfortable. Thirty years ago, I attended a men's seminar with my mentor, Tom Whilhite. I even helped him design parts of the program. During one of the segments I didn't create, he had us filling in holes on his ranch for several days. We'd all paid $7,500 for the seminar, so you can imagine some of the reactions. In addition, we knew that at the first rain, those potholes we'd worked hard to fix would simply reappear. In our minds, the road needed to be paved with some type of blacktop, not just filled in with loose dirt. But what we wanted and how we thought it should be didn't really matter. What counted was serving my mentor and giving him what he desired, whether I understood his logic or not.

It took me some time to come to the realization that service is providing what's wanted, not what I'd like to give. That lesson has served me well over the years and is the mark of a compassionate samurai. You don't even have to understand the meaning or the value of what you're doing. What you need to know is that it matters to the other person—that's what contribution is about. Practice asking your boss what she really wants. Practice with your children, with someone you date, and with a total stranger.

You'll find that some people don't know what they want. Some are embarrassed to tell you, and others may be suspicious of why you want to know, thinking you might take advantage of them. Compassionate samurai are experts at conversing in such a way that people open up and tell them what they want. Expert status doesn't come overnight; it requires repeated practice, so start asking now.

Why People Don't Give

There are five primary reasons why people don't give:

1. They believe that there isn't enough.

2. They're self-centered.

3. They think that others aren't worthy of the gift.

4. They believe they've already given.

5. Their ego tells them that this is really beneath them.

Either/Or Mentality

One thing that often hinders our ability to be lifelong contributors and people of lasting significance is what my good friend Bob "Doctor Increase" Harrison calls the either/or mind-set. This belief is at the very heart of scarcity. A disease of the average man or woman, this mentality is most obvious in the area of finances. People are conditioned or programmed to believe that they must either be spiritual or have money, but not both. Another belief of this type that centers around finances is that we can either have wealth or values—we can have "money or a kind heart" but not both.

In essence, according to this belief, there's only a fixed amount of money available, and a person can either take care of herself or take care of others but not both. Those who have this mind-set might say, "I can either be successful in my job or in my family but not both." Either you're right or I am, but one of us has to be wrong. There's time to do this or time to do that, but there isn't enough to do both. Scarcity thinking suggests you have to make a clear-cut decision between one option and another because there's not enough to go around.

A compassionate samurai knows that he is enough.
Although he isn't the Source, he's connected to the
Source, and he operates from the position of
knowing that there is plenty of everything.

⨯⨯⨯

According to this scarcity line of thinking, there isn't enough money, love, time, good men or women, opportunities, prospects, customers or anything else. This is usually based on the belief that the person isn't enough. A compassionate samurai knows that he *is* enough. Although he isn't the Source, he's connected to the Source—God—and he operates from the position of knowing that there is plenty of everything. (This concept is discussed further in the chapter on abundance.) This is why he always attracts the people, resources, and opportunities he needs.

Most people believe that the more they give away, the less they have. In "fixed-pie" thinking, there's a set amount of something, such as a pie. Every piece you give away means there's less pie. Some games are like that. Service, however, is infinite. There's an unlimited number of ways you can give or contribute. Another issue at the heart of either/or and scarcity thinking is self-centeredness. The problem begins with what we think is reality and who we think we are.

These questions are explored in our seminars and, in some detail, in my books *If How-To's Were Enough, We Would All Be Skinny, Rich & Happy* and *When Good Intentions Run Smack into Reality.* The problem begins with the fact that we believe our eyes, ears, and physical senses define reality. I look at my body and it appears male; my wife's body appears female. I seem to be the more outgoing type while she is shyer. Perhaps I'm on a trip, and it seems at the moment as if her body is in California and mine is in Australia.

From the looks of it, we appear to be separate, so we begin to think that we are our physical selves. Here's the truth: You are not your body; you have a body—that's a *big* difference. The average person thinks she is primarily flesh and bone, and she becomes self-centered in taking care of it. When you realize that you only possess an earthly form and that in a realm you can't see you're connected to others, you become service oriented. When companies hire us to train their staff to work as a team, they sometimes think we're going to create a "bonding" experience, like rafting a river.

There's nothing wrong with that. However, if teamwork is based on that type of chemistry, then when the faces change, the bond breaks. In business, players change all the time, so we can't use that as the standard. When people alter the paradigm of who they are, however, then they can connect with others regardless of who is on the team.

The third reason that prevents people from being huge givers is that they don't feel that others are worthy of the gift. This thinking presupposes that there's some great balance we're trying to maintain, somewhat like the scales of justice. A compassionate samurai isn't about justice; he's about mercy. The former is receiving what you deserve; the latter is receiving what you don't deserve.

The fourth condition that limits giving is that people feel as if they've already contributed. This reasoning is based on an assumption that a certain amount is enough or that they aren't capable of going beyond a certain point. It's like meeting a yearly or monthly quota. A compassionate samurai realizes that the needs are infinite, and because she isn't the source, she has an infinite amount to give.

Never Too Good to Be Involved

Compassionate samurai sometimes get involved in giving on many different levels. Why? Because they're interested in giving what is wanted, not in protecting their image. They don't let their egos interfere with their being of service. They realize more than anyone that if they have a high or lofty position in life, it's directly connected to their ability to serve people. Microsoft, Wal-Mart, Home Depot, and Sears all became major players because they established a precedent of serving people. That's one of the reasons why these companies grew to be such giants.

Beyond financial gain, many of these business warriors realized that they, too, have to be service oriented—even on a personal level. That's why you'll find some of the most successful people in the world offering their time to humanity. They don't just donate their financial resources; they give of their own time and heart. If you're a compassionate samurai CEO of a major corporation, it's nothing for you to be a CEO during the week and then help clean up a low-income inner-city neighborhood on the weekend.

Bill Gates spends his time helping African children fight the war on AIDS, which is destroying their communities. Former president Jimmy Carter is doing the same, assisting sick children in African villages in regaining hope. Oprah Winfrey is "mother" to more than 50,000 children in South Africa, building educational centers, hospitals, and housing for their underprivileged families. Grammy-winning rock star Bono has committed the rest of his life to humanitarian efforts. Nothing is beneath these people.

In fact, it's an honor for them to serve. That's a significant trait of a compassionate samurai.

One time, Tom, my mentor, was hosting a seminar; and Bob, the owner of a very large restaurant chain, was a volunteer on staff. Tom commented that the trash needed to be taken out. Bob immediately did the chore and then proceeded to wash out the trash can! Tom joked later that if he hadn't stopped Bob, the man probably would have painted the can gold. Bob wasn't concerned with ego; taking out the trash wasn't beneath him. He heard a need and he handled it, taking his same attitude of excellence to a mundane task. That's service. That's giving what's wanted and not what we want to give.

Giving What You Have Very Little Of

Compassionate samurai demonstrate their power by what they contribute, not by what they accumulate. Give what you have very little of, not just what you have in abundance. Average people donate what they already have in excess. People who don't have a lot of money sometimes say, "I'll give my time or talent," as if that excuses them from giving money. They're ruled by scarcity. If what's needed is hard for you to manage, that's all the more reason for you to give it. Look at it as if it were a set of weights that you use to work out: The more you do what's hard, the bigger the muscles in that area will be. You will increase your capacity to give.

Giving changes the benefactor
as much as it does the recipient.

How do you get more of what you want? You sow that same commodity. If you're pressed for time, then give some of your day away. Some successful people tend to have very little time to give to humanitarian efforts. As a result, they tend to shrink from those types of service that include personal involvement, and write checks instead. But that doesn't equate to their fullest contribution. They need to give what they have little of in addition to what they have in abundance. Giving changes the benefactor as much as it does the recipient.

If you have a hardened heart, then give some of your heart away. Allowing access to yourself, your vulnerability, or your friendship are amazingly enabling gifts. Sometimes receiving is the best present you can give. It certainly requires greater exposure than traditional giving. When my dad allows me to help him, it's the greatest thing he can do for me. He doesn't need anything, but allowing me to give to him benefits me. He has done so much for me over the years that now I just want to return that love. Some parents see receiving as a weakness, so they don't allow their children to give to them—and that's a shame.

Giving Up to Go Up

Each economic class has a different challenge that centers around giving. In general, I'd say that the middle class is in a comfort zone. Mediocrity is a selfish pursuit. If we're not striving for more because we're comfortable, then we care more about our own condition than we do about others. Our well-being has taken precedence over our ability to contribute. If you see a starving child but you can't provide food, then all you can do is feel sorry for them. This is the state of the average man or woman.

Compassionate samurai are constantly increasing their capacity to give so they can do more. Perhaps you've heard the saying "Be ye hot or be ye cold, but the lukewarm He shall spew out of His mouth." Maybe God wants us to be hotter rather than indifferent or mediocre. In their book, *Why We Want You to Be Rich,* Robert Kiyosaki and Donald Trump discuss extensively the major fallout within the next decade among America's middle class. They suggest there will be two classes: the poor and the rich. They also suggest that being on either side is a matter of choice. It's your decision to educate yourself in the language of finance or to ignore it. The poor will remain so unless they receive a revelation of their God-given potential and realize they don't have to stay that way; it isn't spiritually noble. The rich are already prosperous because they've applied and mastered the science of wealth. They understand the laws that govern abundance and how to use their creativity to manifest a fortune.

Compassionate samurai use money as a vehicle to contribute and to make a difference. It affects the fulfillment in their life, but it's only a means to an end. Some people hold on to their dollars so tightly because they feel that money is their security. Others do so because they're afraid they'll become poor again, and some believe that hoarding is the way to riches.

> A good leader always replaces him-
> or herself with someone who's better.

This isn't to say that middle-class people don't give. An interesting statistic appeared in the U.S. Annual Report released in the year 2000 (these reports are produced every ten years): $200 billion was donated to nonprofit organizations. Of that, 5 percent came from corporations, 7 percent from foundations, and 88 percent from individuals. Of the amount received from individuals, 75 percent was from those earning less than $150,000 per year.

Sometimes we have to give up control in order to grow an organization. At times, in order to move into management, we may have to stop being the star and allow someone else to receive the recognition. Giving doesn't mean you're losing anything, although that's the way the average person sees it. A good leader always replaces him- or herself with someone who's better. One of the things good leaders pass on is their knowledge and training. Average people hoard their skills and information so they're the only ones who know how to do something, and in the process, they lose their jobs.

*Compassionate samurai
anchor reality to their vision.*

Average people anchor their vision to reality.

Chapter Four

FOCUS

*"Tell me what you pay attention to
and I will tell you who you are."*
— José Ortega y Gasset

Focus is the ability to direct your attention, efforts, or activity at a desired direction or object without being distracted. A compassionate samurai can choose to focus on anything and then maintain that concentration. Average people neither initiate such attention nor are they able to maintain it. The amazing attribute of focus is leverage—it takes average talent, small amounts of time, or minimal resources and produces extraordinary results. It is the fulcrum to a lever. Without a doubt, focus is a quality that makes or breaks a compassionate samurai. It is also the deciding factor in whether he'll ever achieve greatness.

Focus leverages power, just as a magnifying glass focuses the power of the sun. The same amount of energy is there with or without the glass. But if the energy is directed through the device, it can produce fire. A laser can cut through six inches of steel with the same amount of power that goes through a 75-watt lightbulb. The difference is focus.

In my book *If How-To's Were Enough, We Would All Be Skinny, Rich & Happy,* I introduced a model of human beings that had three levels: the conscious mind or head, the subconscious mind or heart, and an infinite level I call God. Your conscious mind is the place where choice and thus focus reside. It's important that the magnifying glass (your conscious mind) doesn't get confused and think it's the power of the sun (God). Compassionate samurai remain humble while doing great things because they recognize that they're merely the magnifying glass.

Average people often succumb to three focus-related challenges:

1. They aren't focused because they're either unwilling or unable to focus.

2. They focus on things that make them ineffective.

3. They're focused but are still unaware of what surrounds them.

Let's deal first with the unwillingness or inability to focus. Life is full of distractions, and few individuals really focus. If you ask a group of people to describe their purpose, the majority will stutter, stammer, and say they just don't know. Their lives are unfocused. Ask most people during breakfast what three things they're absolutely going to accomplish that day and they won't be able to tell you. They're just going to work hard and handle what comes up—whatever that is. They're unfocused. Ask most husbands and wives what the focus of their marriage is and you'll most likely be greeted with blank stares.

One reason average people don't learn to focus is that they live under the false assumption that it requires great amounts of effort and will be a strain on them in some way. Most, in fact, are either focused and uptight *or* unfocused and having fun. This pattern relates back to the scarcity mind-set discussed in the last chapter. Compassionate samurai are better able to make wise decisions, think clearly, and have fun when they're focused *and* relaxed.

As I mentioned earlier, my mentor, Tom, held a ten-day men's workshop on a ranch many years ago. About 40 men from all walks of life attended. Some were considered very successful in a worldly sense and some weren't, but they'd all paid $7,500 to participate. At one point, without giving an explanation, Tom asked us to pull $100 out of our wallet. Although I had no idea what he was up to, I knew he was going to demonstrate a valuable life lesson—that was just his nature.

Looking around the group, I saw many different reactions. Some guys just didn't want to do it; they were suspicious. Others were frustrated because they didn't have that much cash on them. Some guys boastfully pulled out their money, mistakenly thinking that their net worth was in direct relation to their self-worth. Others were simply curious. After all the men complied (to the best of their ability), Tom pulled out a rifle.

He then explained the rules of the game. We'd just entered a competition for which the entry fee was $100. We'd each get one minute to fire five rounds at a target.

The best score would take *all* the money, approximately $4,000. I remember thinking, *This is good. I'm ex-military. I've fired a rifle many times, whereas most of these guys have probably never fired a weapon in their lives.* I thought I could win this game.

The first gentleman stood up. Just as he was about to squeeze the trigger, Tom began screaming in his ear. The man jerked the weapon as he fired, wildly missing the target. Tom laughed and said that with only four bullets and 40 seconds left, he might as well give up. He'd never win. The man was stunned. He put the rifle down and walked away, and the next man stood up. Before firing, he looked over at Tom. Tom smiled. The man turned back to face the target, and again just as he was about to fire, our leader started screaming like a wild man. This went on until every person had taken his turn. You can bet that we all screamed loudly in Tom's ears when it was his turn! Finally, we compared all the targets. I'd come in second—not bad, but no money for a prize. Tom had placed first with the best score. Incredibly, most people wandered off, feeling as if they'd been swindled.

I asked Tom what we were supposed to learn. Although I couldn't see the lesson, I knew he always had one. He asked me a simple question: "Are there distractions in life?" The answer to that was easy—of course, there are many. Then he asked another simple question: "Are there money and time pressures in life?" Again I replied yes, still struggling to see the point. He then explained that the game mirrored life. His yelling simulated the distractions: Phone calls disrupt work plans, work interferes with relationships, and problems in relationships interfere with our careers.

Challenges with kids distract us from the romance in our marriage. A serious illness interrupts our plans. *Life is full of distractions.*

The potential loss of $100 versus the potential gain of $4,000 simulated financial pressures. In the physical world, people can downplay this distraction, but *money pressures exist.* It costs money to rent or buy a house. Good schools and higher education are expensive. We have to pay for groceries, let alone trying to fit in with the right clothes or late-model car.

The time limit—one minute for all five shots— simulated the *time pressures* we're all under. We have a conversation with our son or daughter, but we only have a certain amount of time to talk. After that they lose patience and get on with their lives. We make a sales call or have a management meeting, and even with incomplete information, we have a limited amount of time to get the job done or to make the right decision. Time and money pressures are a part of life. They aren't going anywhere.

In case you've never fired a weapon, here's a pointer for you: If you focus on a target but get uptight, you'll miss. If you relax yet are unfocused, you'll still miss. At West Point, upperclassmen screamed in my face while I recited the lessons I was required to memorize. Although I didn't understand what they were trying to teach me at the time, I was learning to be relaxed and focused at the same time. That rigorous training helped me come in second place in Tom's little game—he was just better at it than I was.

No matter how many distractions come your way, or how much financial or temporal stress you experience, if you have concentrated focus and stay relaxed, you'll hit the bull's-eye every time. That's one of the practices of a compassionate samurai. It's also one of the reasons I love the game of golf. I can practice being relaxed and focused. The ball goes much farther and more accurately when I relax and focus than when I tighten up and try to use force. It's almost counterintuitive to let the club do the work.

One of my good friends, Doug Firebaugh, is considered a guru and an outstanding trainer in the home-based network-marketing industry because of the results he has produced and the tens of thousands of people he has helped (**www.passionfire.com**). Every Christmas, Doug's training addresses the fact that often the network-marketing business slows down during the holidays, when it should be accelerating since everybody is in the buying mood. The average person relaxes with the festivities and becomes unfocused. So Doug walks his people through how they can relax yet focus and significantly increase their business with ease. He uses the very same principle, and it works.

Focusing on Ineffective Things

What's the point of your life? Why are you on Earth? Knowing the answers to these questions helps you focus your life. These are important issues for you to address if you're to have this trait. Then it's a matter of not allowing the many distractions of life to sway you from your purpose. *Compassionate samurai focus on service or contribution, regardless of their circumstances.* Average people focus on themselves and really don't care what happens to others. How much money can I make? How good can I feel in a relationship? How do I look?

Compassionate samurai focus on service or contribution, regardless of their circumstances.

When average people consider others, it's only to ensure that they have more, feel better, and are ahead of the pack. Some of the greatest leaders of our time—such as Mohandas Gandhi; Martin Luther King, Jr.; Nelson Mandela; and Mother Teresa—endured unusual pressure. What these compassionate samurai had in common is that each of them continued to focus on their vision for a better world for everyone. They never wavered. They stayed grounded and centered despite incredible stress.

These leaders endured torture, their families' lives were threatened, they didn't have money to fund their projects, and they withstood public ridicule. No matter what's going on around them, compassionate samurai stay true to their focus because they know that even the slightest distraction could cost many others their destinies. Some people try to get themselves off the hook by thinking that this level of focus only happens on such a great level with special people. But you, too, can be a compassionate samurai.

One of the ways in which compassionate samurai stay focused is to keep death in their minds all the time. Before you start thinking that's morbid, follow this line of reasoning: These individuals live every day as if it were their last, so they experience life to the fullest. Confronting your own mortality alleviates the fear of death and lends clarity of purpose to what life is about. By pretending they have at least 75 years to live, average people dilute the intensity of their existence.

In his book *The Code of the Samurai: A Modern Translation of the Bushido Shoshinshu of Taira Shigesuke*, Thomas Cleary writes:

> One who is supposed to be a warrior considers it his foremost concern to keep death in mind at all times, every day and every night, from the morning of New Year's Day through the night of New Year's Eve.
>
> As long as you keep death in mind at all times, you will also fulfill the ways of loyalty and familial duty. You will also avoid myriad evils and calamities, you will be physically sound and healthy, and you will live a long life. What is more, your character will improve and your virtue will grow.

Then he continues:

> When you assume that your stay in this world will last, various wishes occur to you, and you become very desirous. You want what others have, and cling to your own possessions, developing a mercantile mentality.

Cleary suggests that keeping death in mind is the treatment for covetousness and greed, among a host of other evils. The purpose is not to get you to run out and pick out your favorite casket. Rather, it's to encourage you to live your life with a sense of purpose and urgency. If today were the last day of your life, how would you spend it? Who would you be a blessing to? What kind of support system would you set up for your loved ones? Would you talk to an old friend, or would you be sure to tell someone that you loved him or her? Would you seek a spiritual path that you've always dreamed of?

If today were the last day of your life,
how would you spend it?

Whatever the case may be, you'd live free of the mundane affairs that have proven to be little more than distractions. When you live with death in mind, you're not trying to preserve your life and simply survive, because you know it's a lost cause. You play full-out because you don't have anything to lose.

Forgetting: The Key to Focusing on the Effective Things

I'm writing this part of the book on an airplane after conducting one of our one-evening Champions Workshops in Detroit. A woman came up to me at the end of the session and passionately explained how much she wanted to attend our weekend event called Personal Mastery, but she just couldn't afford it.

I asked, "What ideas have you come up with to create any money?" She responded that she hadn't come up with any. Notice that she was passionate and had lots of energy. What was her problem? Her focus was in the wrong direction. She was concentrating on her problem and not on a solution.

71

This woman's trouble—that she had no money—was a condition of her past. She needed to forget her problem and her past. With no focus on a working solution, it was little wonder she had no answers. Average people ask, "Can I?" They base their answer on what's already happened. Compassionate samurai ask a different question: "How can I?" Even if they apply no more energy, because this question has a different focus, it has enormously different results.

Try it out in your own life. Pick something that you've decided you can't do for some reason—you don't have the time or money or maybe you can't get a babysitter. Perhaps it's buying a house, losing 20 pounds, or getting a new job. Write it down. Commit now to spending an hour solving that problem.

What was your experience? If you're an average reader, you just blew by that last sentence. You're waiting for me to tell you what your experience most likely was. Do yourself a favor: Put down this book and spend an hour solving whatever problem you decided you couldn't solve.

Compassionate samurai don't get to their level by just reading. They take action. They have to fight some battles and spend the time training.

Consider this as part of your education in learning to focus. Now, what was *your* experience? Did you have some resistance to even doing it? That's an inability to focus. A compassionate samurai can make a decision to concentrate on anything and then is able to maintain it. In our Personal Mastery seminar, we have people practice the art and skill of focusing. And it's not just a matter of being focused or not. We try to get people to realize what they're focusing on.

I used to include an exercise in which people break one-inch thick boards with their bare hands. Their ability to complete the task isn't a matter of muscle, but rather of concentrated focus. The first time we did that exercise, my wife was adamantly against it. That was fine, since our seminars concentrate on personal choice. The focus is on "learning," and many times participants will discover as much or even more by not doing an exercise as they would have by participating.

Then my wife saw a petite 13-year-old girl break the board. She recognized that the exercise wasn't about strength, so she mustered up the courage and did it herself. We put the broken board in a very nice frame and hung it in our home. Every time she looks at the display, it triggers her to focus and appreciate how powerful she is when she's concentrating. One event that occurred immediately as a result was that she headed up a spaghetti dinner fundraiser for the PTA at our child's school. Until that point, she'd always been a volunteer, but she was never willing to be responsible as the leader. By forgetting her past self-image, she produced the most successful event of this kind that the PTA had ever experienced.

Focus can overcome incredible odds by developing its own odds. Tiger Woods is probably the best golfer alive today—he may be the best of all time. One of the skills that makes him a compassionate samurai is his ability to forget. I've seen him strike a ball off the fairway into the woods. Incredibly, on his very next shot, he'll make the green. He forgets each shot after taking seven steps.

The average person would be beating himself up for the next ten strokes and ruin his score by compounding the problem. Tiger is able to put each shot out of his mind and hit the next one as a fresh start. This idea applies in all areas of life. Can you forget the time your spouse neglected your anniversary and didn't get you a card, let alone a gift? If so, you can have an incredible marriage. Unable to forget, the average person focuses on the problem. What's the worst thing you've ever done? Can you forget it? If you can't do that, can you at least allow it to become neutral so that it doesn't affect your life?

Compassionate samurai can forget. I've seen thousands of people allow their past to plague their future. Years after a certain tragic event occurs, they just can't seem to let it go. They allow the negativity of their painful history to become their everyday reality. As long as you allow your past to haunt you, you'll never be free to pursue your future. You won't even be able to focus on your present.

Compassionate samurai forget their
successes as well as their failures!

Are you familiar with the Paul in the Bible? This is a great example of forgetting. Paul wrote more than two-thirds of the New Testament. He was educated under Gamaliel, a law professor, and he left this tutelage with honors and distinctions. Yet Paul readily confesses that he doesn't know everything. That's a salient point. *Compassionate samurai forget their successes as well as their failures!* The average person holds onto their victories and forfeits even more spectacular achievements.

Never let your good get in the way of your spectacular. Paul had a terrible past: He'd persecuted, tortured, and even beheaded Christ's followers. How could he become a disciple? There was only one way: He had to forget. Failing to remember things frees us to focus on something new. Compassionate samurai never let what matters most suffer for the things that matter least. They focus on what's most important.

Suffering is optional; pain is not. *Suffering is the unnecessary prolongation of a painful experience by remaining focused on that pain.*

Be Here Now

In our Personal Mastery workshops, we teach an old concept called "Be here now," which is related to focus. This concept means that your body, feelings, spirit, and thoughts are all at the same place at the same time. Have you ever been physically at home but your mind was still at work? That's not being here now. Have you ever done a job but your heart wasn't in it? That's not being here now. *Not being here now kills effectiveness and intimacy.* The average person isn't disciplined mentally to be here now.

Not being here now kills effectiveness and intimacy.

∽∾

When average people have a problem, they continue to focus on the problem instead of being here now to create a solution. Have you ever seen a deer frozen in a car's headlights? Often the car hits the deer because the deer can't get out of the way. It focused on the wrong thing—the headlights—so it became distracted from the here-and-now. The deer could easily outmaneuver the car, but focusing on the wrong thing caused it to become paralyzed by circumstances. That's the story of the average person's life. Compassionate samurai never allow circumstances to impair their focus on what's important.

Focused but Not Blind

Some people insist that focusing would cause them to "miss out" on too many other things. Have you ever known people who are so focused on their work that they ignore their family? Of course you have. This mind-set actually confuses two concepts. It is an outgrowth of both the scarcity and the either/or mentalities. *Compassionate samurai are focused, but they are still aware of everything going on around them.* That is a skill to develop. In aikido, for example, your opponent can throw a punch and you must be focused on responding to that punch, but you must also be aware of what is going on around you. Although two things are happening simultaneously, it is considered singularity of focus. It's very possible that there may be another threat behind you. Are there other people in the vicinity? Are they friendly?

I'm known in my family and at work for my strong ability to focus. My ability to maintain 360-degree awareness is something I've had to work on. If I'm focused on driving and my children pass by on the opposite side of the road in their car and wave at me, I'll never see them.

Perhaps the funniest example was one October. I'd flown in on a red-eye and then driven home from the airport. It was about 7 A.M. when I arrived. I joined my wife and daughter shortly before my daughter left for school. Roma asked me if I wanted an early Christmas present. I said, "No, I'd would rather wait." She giggled that we might have a problem. I didn't understand what was going on, so Roma told me to go back into the living room. To my surprise, there was a 54-inch wide-screen color television with a bow wrapped around it.

Now, I had passed through the living room at least three times drinking a cup of coffee and thinking. I was so focused on my thoughts that I never saw the television. How can you miss a 54-inch TV? By being focused on something else. When my family wants to have fun with me, they call me the "King of Awareness." What 54-inch TV opportunities have you missed because you either weren't focused or you *were* focused but you lacked an awareness of what was going on around you?

Many men are so focused on their professional life that they're blind to family problems that develop. The key is not to be driven by scarcity and make either/or choices, but to do both. In the beginning, you may have to practice focusing on what's in front of you and then switch. In other words, you focus on work when you're at work and on home when you're at home. Focusing on one problem at work with one manager, and then ten minutes later, take all your thought, and focus on a totally different issue with a different person.

The speed with which you can shift your focus is an ability you want to spend time developing. It will effectively mobilize your power and creativity, but it's still only one step on the way to being simultaneously focused and having 360-degree awareness. During the next conversation you have with someone, focus on the person's words. That alone can be *very* difficult. Most people are so focused on what they want to say that they're anxiously looking for an opening in which to say it. As a result, they don't really hear what the other person is saying.

Or they may be distracted by a family crisis and are thinking about that as the other person is talking. As you learn to be focused on "what they're saying," learn to increase your 360-degree awareness. You will become aware of not just what the other person is saying, but what he or she is feeling. You will also be able to feel what they're *not* saying—and that's important. You'll become aware of what's going on with the person who's sitting next to the person you're talking to, and they haven't even said anything. You'll become aware of the overall energy in the room.

*Compassionate samurai say what
they mean and mean what they say.*

*Average people are honest
when it's convenient.*

Chapter Five

HONESTY

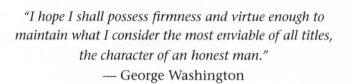

*"I hope I shall possess firmness and virtue enough to
maintain what I consider the most enviable of all titles,
the character of an honest man."*
— George Washington

If you took a random survey of a thousand people and
asked them if they thought they were honest, the
majority would answer, "Why of course I'm honest." Most
people really think they are. If you ask a crook, he'd say
he's honest. He'd probably say, "I tell people that I'm going
to steal from them, and that's being honest." As crazy as it
sounds, that's how some people think. People have mental
filters concerning honesty.

The average person's favorite saying is "Yeah I'm
honest, but—" Remember, it's always the phrase that starts
with *but* that houses the lie you're living and covering up.
Genuine honesty isn't hidden or diluted. There really are
no ifs, ands, or buts. The truth is the truth. Since most
people have become desensitized to dishonesty, they have
difficulty recognizing when they're being dishonest.

We've established our own set of rules concerning what's honest from what's not. When we're confronted with a situation, we escape the truth with a prefabricated "exception clause" that we've become comfortable using. "I'm honest, but taxes are another issue." That's just one of millions of lies people feel comfortable with.

When I went to West Point, there was a honor code: If you lie, cheat, or steal, or *tolerate anyone who does,* the cadets threw you out of West Point. That was pretty straightforward; I knew they weren't joking.

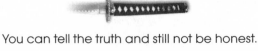

You can tell the truth and still not be honest.

Because I didn't want to get kicked out of the academy, I didn't lie, cheat, or steal while I was there, so I really thought that I was honest. Only later in life did I realize that I needed to check myself in the area of honesty. *You can tell the truth and still not be honest.* Honesty isn't about successfully getting through an incident or two. Honesty is a lifestyle. It's not something that you do once in a while; it's who you *are.* Compassionate samurai are honest not only when it's convenient to be so but at all times, even if it costs their life or when no one is around.

The Acceptable Lie

Once in a seminar with my mentor, Tom had us mill around the room telling the other participants what really mattered to us that we wanted to achieve. I told the others that I wanted to be more organized at work. I *did* want that. I wasn't lying, but I wasn't being totally honest. What really mattered to me, what I really wanted, was a wildly romantic, long-lasting relationship. But there was no way that I was going to say that to strangers, much less to people I knew. People thought I had it together, and I was afraid of what they might think if I told them the truth.

Being organized was a more acceptable response. I began to see that although I wouldn't lie, there were plenty of times in business and personal relationships where I didn't disclose the full truth. There are many ways a lack of honesty can show up. A person may become accustomed to telling people what he thinks they want to hear. When he does this, he's really hiding. He's not only hiding the total truth, but he's also hiding a piece of himself that he really doesn't want others to know. It's the side that so few people want to reveal to others. It could be motivated by fear or maybe even pride.

Whatever the motivation, some people use persuasive words to hide the real issue. Although they don't feel as if they're being dishonest, they are. For compassionate samurai, honesty isn't about giving people what they want to hear or even what sounds acceptable. Rather, it's about giving people the truth, the whole truth, and nothing but the truth. When people hide their truest intentions and always tell people what they want them to hear, it does a disservice both to the person who's speaking and to the one who's listening.

The Many Faces of Lying

Dishonesty shows up in many different ways. Just because people tell the truth under favorable conditions doesn't mean they aren't lying. There are some things that people tend to do and they don't even realize they're being dishonest.

This section isn't just about exposing your lies. It's far more about revelation, in the sense of self-discovery. There are some things that you may not know about yourself; once revealed, these insights might shed a clearer light on you. I'm listing the ways to be dishonest here to help you understand some of the ways in which you can make a more gallant effort to be honest, even in unfavorable conditions.

There are several ways to be dishonest:

1. Telling someone something that isn't true. This is the most obvious way to be dishonest. Perhaps you've heard stories about the Vietnam War, when body counts were highly inflated to give the information that upper management wanted. The person telling the lie *knows* it's a lie. Managers will tell their boss that they'll make something happen even when they know they can't. Salespeople promise unrealistic results just to make a sale. People engage in this form of lying to make themselves look good, to be accepted, to avoid negative consequences, or to get people off their back.

2. Giving the illusion of what is not so. People who make cold calls to sell services might tell their boss, "I made 20 calls." In reality, they talked to ten people and left ten messages. They know that talking to ten people represents their reality and the number of people they actually called. In theory, they can call a thousand people and speak with no one—so really they haven't called anyone. They've given the illusion of having done something that they have not.

One way to deal with this behavior is to have an agreement and clear language. In other words, what does it really mean to call 20 people? At Klemmer & Associates, we enroll people for our seminars at various levels. What does it mean to enroll someone? All our employees receive training in the language we use and the definition of certain words. The language of enrollment is not those who fill out a piece of paper. The enrolled are those who have paid in full and specified a date of attendance. A deposit doesn't count. A form with no money doesn't count. The specificity of the language assists in telling the truth.

3. Not telling what is so. One of the main reasons why people are dishonest is that they don't want to look bad. Withholding the truth is also dishonest. I'm not suggesting that you air your dirty laundry to everybody you meet. You have to use wisdom. But if you're withholding information with the intent to escape consequences, that, too, is just as dishonest as straightforward lying.

4. Pretending not to know. What are you ignoring in your marriage or in your business? It's there, but you subconsciously act as if it's not. Honesty with yourself is as important as honesty with other people. You're not fooling yourself. You're delaying your own progress by holding yourself back with things you know aren't true, even if no one else knows. You know you know, so why not just say it? Don't try to fool anyone, because in time you'll be the one who is fooled. Many average people never prepare a cash-flow statement or an asset-and-liability statement because they don't want to know what it will reveal. Not preparing these statements allows them to pretend not to know—but they do.

Transparency vs. Honesty

There *is* a difference between transparency and honesty. Transparency is when everything is easily seen. There is always a reason for honesty, but there's not always wisdom in transparency. There are times when transparency is needed, and other times when you may want to refrain from being too transparent.

For example, if you had an affair 20 years ago and you no longer live that lifestyle, transparency about the matter would be unnecessary. A compassionate samurai wouldn't do that. Talking about it might relieve your guilt, but it could harm the person you're with. On the other hand, if you were asked whether you had an affair, honesty would require your answering it truthfully despite it being uncomfortable. The objective of a samurai is "to serve." Transparency should be about helping someone else to conquer an area that you've also conquered. Transparency has a very definite purpose. Let's look at the definitions from *Webster's Dictionary:*

- *Transparent*—(a) free from pretense or deceit, FRANK; (b) easily detected or seen through, OBVIOUS; (c) readily understood; (d) characterized by visibility or accessibility of information, especially concerning business practices.

- *Honesty*—(a) fairness and straightforwardness of conduct; (b) adherence to the facts, SINCERITY; INTEGRITY implies trustworthiness and incorruptibility to a degree that one is incapable of being false to a trust, responsibility, or pledge.

According to this definition, honesty has to do with integrity and trustworthiness, while transparency means making yourself visible so you can be better understood. At times, people shy away from both honesty and transparency because they're afraid. With honesty, most people always have to weigh the consequences. People tend to chicken out because they don't want to get yelled at or fired. Let's look at Enron, for example. In this case, employees didn't expose the people they knew were engaging in criminal activities for fear of losing their jobs.

Have no illusions—there are harmful consequences to being honest. It's why the average person won't be honest. However, what is the cost of not being honest? Usually, it's the loss of intimacy, efficiency, and aliveness. First, lying destroys the trust the other person has in you. Once you lie, the veracity of everything you say is in doubt. Relationships and businesses are based on trust. Thus, you destroy intimacy in relationships and make business inefficient and slow.

Second, every time you violate your own principles, it's like taking a knife and cutting yourself. A piece of you dies. It doesn't matter what principle you violate. You become less whole; you compromise your integrity. That's why there are a lot of 40- to 50-year-old walking zombies in this world. They exist, but they're not really alive, and you can see it. The average person undervalues transparency, realness, and authenticity.

The people who were involved in the Enron scandal weren't transparent, because transparency would have revealed something about them that they wanted to hide. Most people have something that they would rather others not know. That's not a problem. You don't have to tell the world everything. But there are times when telling someone else frees you and others. That is the right time to be transparent.

People will only follow competency and image so far, but they'll follow leaders who are transparent and genuine almost anywhere. Their transparency gives people a sense of certainty in tough times. The network-marketing or multilevel industry is one of the niches we support. It's a phenomenal industry whose reputation has been tarnished by people who haven't been honest. Because honor is one of their most dearly held traits, compassionate samurai would never allow their industry's reputation to be negatively affected by their behavior, or the behavior of anyone else.

The Rich "Big-Time" Liar

A lack of honesty can show up in many ways. Some people buy expensive cars, fine clothes, and luxurious houses to make themselves feel successful. This lifestyle also draws people to them. That is deceitful. At times, people buy things they can't afford because they know how powerful *image* is. Image is really what sells people in the short term. Don't tell people that you're making big money if you aren't. Let them know that you're in the *process* of making money.

I'll admit that it doesn't sound really inviting to tell 100 or so fresh prospects that you're saving up for a Lexus, and in about ten months—just from the proceeds of your network-marketing business—you should have enough money to buy it. That doesn't usually sell as quickly. But it may if you try it. That approach may surprise a few people—okay it will shock everybody. But people will have a great deal of respect for your honesty. Honesty breeds trust, and trust is essential for a business.

So what if you don't have the Mercedes-Benz and the big waterfront estate with a yacht. You have honesty, and that goes much further than material things. Traditional samurai used things for their benefit, that's all. They never defined themselves by the things they used. They only saw those things as tools.

When a person defines himself by possessions, that process is never-ending because things age. They no longer have the flair they once had. And when that defines you, you'll always have to keep up an image just to please others.

The image is not you. It's a reflection of very low self-esteem. For the most part, these people are very seldom transparent or honest. They dread someone finding out that they're not who they say they are and that they've been living a lie for many years. Leading by image shows that you're not very interested in going through the process that will genuinely afford you the finer things of life. It takes time and commitment to realize your dream. It may not happen overnight, but that's all right. The process is so valuable that you need to savor every moment.

Remember that a samurai sword requires 80,000 folds and is heated and beaten repeatedly before it's ready to be presented for use. Maybe before *you* are presented for show or use, you need to be beaten 80,000 times, too. I'm speaking figuratively here, but I hope you're getting the point. Your image is constantly being made. Don't try to become everything overnight. Give it time and be honest in your process. Make small steps, celebrate each step, and people will honor that quality in you.

What's Your Dirty Little Secret?

In his book *Winning,* Jack Welch calls "lack of candor" the biggest dirty little secret in business. He writes:

> What a huge problem it is. Lack of candor basically blocks smart ideas, fast action, and good people from contributing all the stuff they've got. It's a killer. When you've got candor—and you'll probably never completely get it, mind you—everything just operates faster and better.

I agree with Jack. He is perhaps the most successful CEO in American history. If anyone knows about honesty in business and how it affects overall success, it's Jack Welch. Honesty helps make things flow smoother. Dishonesty slows the progress of organizational development, family growth, personal growth, and even mental expansion.

Be honest with yourself. Where can you improve? Are there areas where you need to grow? Where could you act or take actions far more maturely than you have in the past? Evaluate yourself and give yourself a grade. Be honest. Tell yourself what areas could use a complete overhaul. Samurai don't want people around who are always going to agree with them. They want to surround themselves with people who will confront them frankly about areas where they need to improve, which will help them grow and prosper.

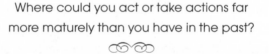

Where could you act or take actions far
more maturely than you have in the past?

Why Be Honest? Because You Care

Why would a person want to be honest in marriage or in business? What are the benefits? I mentioned that honesty makes you more efficient. One of the other primary reasons to be honest is because you care. If you don't care about anybody or anything, then honesty won't matter much to you.

What if your child asks if you've ever used drugs? Should you lie to them as a preventive measure? Absolutely not! Don't tell your kids a lie. Tell the truth. Tell them that you used them and why you regret it. It's better to be honest and show you care than to have people discover things about you. You may wonder, *Do I have to reveal everything?* There's no need to go into detail. That will only aggravate the situation. Tell enough to show you're being honest; by doing so, you're honoring the other person. This honesty develops trust and closeness.

Even though you care, honesty can complicate a friendship, a marriage, and a business. It makes things messy. Couples have been married for decades and they're not honest with each other about sexual likes and dislikes. Being honest presents a minefield of possible hurt feelings. Average people would rather avoid the discomfort of negotiating that minefield than be honest and deal with the situation. They trade closeness for comfort. You've probably been taught that no one is hurt by a "white lie." That's not true—and you know it. At times, others realize it's not true, too.

I'm not saying that you can use honesty as an excuse to be cruel. Find a way to tell the truth and honor the other person. For example, two people in a relationship may have different expectations. Perhaps one sees it as a permanent relationship. Perhaps the other person is just going along for the ride, and it's simply a relationship of convenience. The average person is afraid of losing what he has and either avoids the conversation or is very vague. Perhaps he likes the benefits: gifts, dinners, nights out on the town.

It's not honest to continue this relationship without dealing with the situation. One person may want to say, "Let's slow down. We're going too fast in this relationship." But perhaps he's afraid that saying what he feels will jeopardize the benefits he's receiving from the relationship.

That really doesn't matter. Complications will come either sooner or later. Compassionate samurai honor the other person and the principle of honesty by declaring where they are in a relationship.

A whole society can collectively be dishonest. For many years, Americans turned a blind eye to the damages of segregation. Today, many people are turning a blind eye to the effects of environmental damage or the deterioration of our schools. Some people who are very overweight or in poor health aren't being honest with themselves. They convince themselves that they can continue to eat anything, anytime, and anywhere, and they'll be fine.

In time, that attitude will catch up with them and they'll die. The sooner they deal with it, the better their chances of survival are. That goes for all areas of life. Prevention is always the best method for dealing with things. Compassionate samurai deal with issues before they arise and before they get out of hand. You will only use preventive measures when you sincerely and wholeheartedly care about yourself and the people who care about you.

Honesty, a Two-Edged Sword

Most people are generally not prepared for the repercussions of honesty. That is why they tend to shy away from it. Being honest is like paying with cash instead of using a credit card. With cash, you pay the little prices up-front and suffer some discomfort. With a credit card, you live an illusion of comfort until you have to pay the bill, and then you suffer depression.

Honesty is much like a two-edge sword. It can cut, but it can also mend. That's the power of the sword. Often things have to be cut before they can start to heal. It's not always comfortable, but it's effective. There are benefits to honesty that you will receive when you choose the compassionate samurai's path.

1. Honesty increases intimacy. If I want a relationship to be a deep, meaningful relationship, that will only come through honesty. Intimacy means *in-to-me I see.* If I want intimacy, honesty is a must.

2. Honesty brings more people and their creativity into the process. When I was honest with what I was working on within myself, other people started to become more honest, too. In the workplace, if I'm looking for a greater commitment from people, I'll be honest. They'll be more committed than complaining.

3. Honesty speeds things up. It takes the clutter out of events. It saves time and makes things more efficient.

Using Diplomacy

Here's a final word: Don't use the principle of honesty to justify being obnoxious and to make people feel less than human. Use tact. It's not beneficial to berate people just because you notice an area in which they may need improvement. Did you even ask their permission to give them feedback? In our company, I've heard conversations in which one person says, "May I give you some feedback?" The other person responds, "No, I have other things on my mind, and I won't hear it. Please give it to me tomorrow." What a great, honest conversation!

If someone agrees to receive feedback, there's always a way to say what you need to say without being rude and impolite. Be aware that your criticism of others frequently says more about you than it does about them. *You can only criticize in others that which reflects your own experience. You can only identify in others the things that are easily detected in you.* The only difference between them and you is that their issue is noticeable and yours is concealed.

You can only criticize in others that which reflects your own experience. You can only identify in others the things that are easily detected in you.

Qualify your intentions before approaching the person. What do you want to accomplish? Be honest about your intentions. Do you really want to help the other person, or just make them feel bad? If your intention is the latter, keep your suggestions to yourself, regardless of whether they're honest or not. There's always a certain way to approach a matter. If you really want to help, the way you handle a situation will determine the outcome. What you may have intended for good can be obscured and turn out poorly because you went about it the wrong way.

Use your mind and better judgment before entering a situation that involves your honesty toward someone else. In fact, your most honest observations are usually about you. Master that first before trying those skills on other people. Many people have been taught how to say the "right" things in various situations. But just saying the right things cannot cover up the real you. Your real desire will always be revealed. So, it's much better to deal honestly up-front. If you don't, your true desires and motives will be exposed in time. There really aren't any secrets.

When that happens, you'll look bad, and the other person will pretty much have lost faith in your word because you told him what he wanted to hear. Perhaps a building contractor gives a client what he wants to hear. He says, "The work will be finished in a month." When the job winds up taking two months to complete, the client is angry. The contractor is scared and frustrated, knowing that he may be sued for breach of contract. He told the customer what he wanted to hear, yet he didn't intend to follow through. This happens all of the time.

Say what you'll do and do what you say. The average person will say something like "I'll try to—" It is the illusion of commitment. *Trying is lying.* Having an exit door in place just in case something doesn't go as expected is avoiding the truth. You can't get into something, expecting it to go sour. If you do, that's exactly what will happen. Many people marry with the intention of escaping if something goes wrong. They commit to each other with vows (giving each other what they and the attendees want to hear with less-than-honest intentions).

The point is that no matter what you say, everybody will know where your heart is in time. The cure is to be honest. Contractors, let your client know up-front that you're working on a big job three towns over and that you took her job to keep revenue flowing so you can meet payroll. Let him know that it may take longer than normal, perhaps two or three months to complete the job, but you'll throw in some extras for his patience. Your honesty may lose some customers, but it will attract many others.

And before you say "I do," have an honest talk about all of the things that might cause you to hit the road early on. "If this happens, I'm not going to stick around. I'm gone!" Okay, that's pretty blunt, but at least it's honest. Your fiancé may not want to hear that, but he'll appreciate it in the long run. After all of the talk, your truth—as seen in your behavior—is the only thing people will see. Traditional samurai didn't use many words. They were relatively quiet people. It's not that they couldn't talk; it's just that they understood the power of words and didn't want to use them flippantly. The samurai realized that silence would cause them to take action, at times quicker than words.

∽∾

*Compassionate samurai hold
principles above personal benefit.*

*Average people do whatever
is best for themselves.*

Chapter Six

HONOR

"Integrity is the essence of everything successful."
— Unknown

To honor someone is to hold that person in high esteem and respect. Every major religion has a tenet to hold parents in high esteem, yet dishonor runs rampant in our society. People don't understand the importance of honoring others, even at a very basic level. Children dishonor their parents. Some children lie to their parents; others swear at and are openly rebellious in front of them. Athletes spit at each other and hit referees. Officials turn a blind eye toward steroid use, imposing only token penalties.

Taunting became so commonplace that it had to be specified as a penalty. Politicians think nothing of throwing "dirt" at an opponent—it's considered part of the game. Nobody expects politicians to tell the truth. Lawyers are held in low esteem because they're known for doing whatever it takes regardless of principles. Remember the old adage "Honor among thieves." Kids are joining gangs for honor because they can't find it anyplace else.

A couple years ago, a member of the Dixie Chicks, a country-singing group, made some derogatory remarks about President Bush. Tens of thousands of Americans trashed their CDs in response. Amazingly, in the interviews that ensued, the lead singer couldn't understand that reaction. She thought these people didn't respect freedom of speech. In reality, very few people had an issue with her antiwar sentiment. Half the country disagrees with the President. They were reacting to her calling the President names. Dishonor always carries a very high price. It costs the person who is dishonored, and it also costs everyone affiliated with the one who engaged in the dishonoring behavior.

The price to be paid for dishonor isn't always immediately recognized. But that doesn't mean that it isn't paid. Society tends to hide the effects and consequences of dishonor, the thinking being that if you don't show honor you can get away with it. The truth is that this will never happen. It will catch up to you sooner or later. A person who understands honor understands that in honoring the person you're dealing with, you are essentially honoring yourself, your family, your work group, and any other affiliation you have, even the samurai name. The traditional samurai even honored their enemies.

Honoring Whomever You Interact With

I asked a high-level executive friend, Tim Redmond, to come in for a couple of days, observe me, and let me know what adjustments I needed to make to lead a company earning $100 million a year. Part of his feedback was a comment that floored me. He said, on the one hand, that I had a vision that inspired him, empowered others, saw the best in them, and paid them more than he would. On the other hand, I was condescending toward my employees. I was shocked.

Perhaps I was in gross denial because I never saw myself as being condescending toward *anyone,* especially my employees. I asked him to explain in greater detail. He asked me to recall the conversations I'd had throughout the day with people in the office. I reflected. He then said I hadn't had any conversations; I'd basically had monologues. I'd told people what to do instead of asking their opinion. Not giving people a chance to offer their viewpoints on what needed to be done is condescending. It didn't honor their value as Klemmer & Associates teammates.

Since then, I've been working on starting every conversation with a question. That's an honoring behavior. It basically says that I value someone's input. Asking Tim to give me feedback was an honoring behavior to him and to myself. I've now asked my employees to tell me when I forget to start off a conversation with a question. That's another honoring behavior. You can be honest without being condescending or belittling. But the first way to do this is by hearing them out.

When compassionate samurai communicate with others,
their highest goal is to be a listener.

As simple as this lesson may sound, it's a very big problem for a lot of people, especially controllers and high achievers. At times, high achievers feel as if they've earned the right not to listen to anyone else since they've already "arrived." Nothing could be further from the truth. The higher up you go in life, the more input you're going to need regularly to stay there. You may have heard the adage "The bigger they are the harder they fall." I'd much rather listen to others' advice and instruction and preserve the fruits of my labor than to lose it all through arrogance and pride.

When compassionate samurai communicate with others, their highest goal is to be a listener. Intent listening shows that you honor the person with whom you're communicating. And, of course, you always learn far more through listening than you'll ever learn by talking— perhaps that's why God gave us two ears and only one mouth. Keeping your agreements with others, even when they appear to be small, is a mark of honor. Showing up on time whether it's for a meeting or coming home from work is an honoring behavior.

Average people think nothing of being late. It communicates that what they have to do is more important than what anyone else has to do. I've seen executives repeatedly keep a hundred people waiting. That is dishonoring behavior. Simply speaking well of other people is honoring. Some people don't ever give anyone else credit for anything; that behavior is dishonoring. Think about your boss or someone up the line in your business. When was the last time you built that person up to someone else? Perhaps you're thinking that there's nothing to edify.

There's always something good to find in someone else, whether it's sincerity, determination, or joyful spirit. Perhaps you think some people don't deserve it. That's even more reason to edify and honor them. Sow honor into them without them even knowing. It will make you look good. What can you do to honor your children? What *do* you do? Most important, what *will* you do? Do you give them one-on-one time? Do you ask their opinions? Are they encouraged to participate in conversations with adults? Do you allow them to solve their problems, or are you always solving their problems for them?

I frequently talk about my mentor, Tom. I tell people that my life is different because of him. I wouldn't be a best-selling author, I wouldn't have raised millions of dollars for causes I believe in, I wouldn't be married, I wouldn't be a Christian, and on and on if Tom hadn't come into my life. It's been 24 years since he was killed, but it's part of what I do to honor him. Like most people, he had his faults; some were pretty severe. I never mention those. I talk about *my* faults instead. There's no way I can ever repay him, but this is the right thing to do.

That is what compassionate samurai do. How many times have you heard someone complain about his or her organization? Compassionate samurai never do that. They will go to the person or to management and

103

register a complaint. That actually honors them because it says they care enough about the organization to go to someone who can do something about the situation. They never complain to people who *can't* do anything about the situation. Average people complain to whoever will listen.

How can you honor the organization you work for? You can speak well of it. You can look out for it. Abusing an expense account dishonors the company that pays you and your co-workers. Leaving a communal kitchen at work a mess dishonors the company and your co-workers. Average people do what's best for themselves, regardless of the impact on others. Average people make a sale whether it's good for the other person or not. Average people increase their income and lifestyle, even if it pollutes the environment. Compassionate samurai wouldn't dishonor future generations.

How can you honor the service people you interact with every day? These people include waiters, retail salesclerks, janitors, or bank tellers. Do you know their names and use them? People love it when a customer uses their name. Customers expect that as part of good service. The average person doesn't return the honoring behavior, although it's so easy and simple to do. Do you ignore the people who serve you, or do you ask a question or two that honors them and contributes to their day? What kind of tips do you leave?

What tone of voice do you use when you're at the airport and there's a delay? Compassionate samurai always look to serve and to honor other human beings. You may have heard about the practice of tithing and giving the first 10 percent of your earnings to God or to wherever you get your spiritual nourishment. Tithing is an honoring practice. It is an acknowledgment that God is the source of all things, rather than our own intellect or skills. This behavior honors God.

Compassionate samurai always look to
serve and to honor other human beings.

Honoring Yourself

Honor is really about respect. The word *respect* is commonly used as it relates to respecting others. For example, "Respect your elders. Honor your mother and your father. Give honor to whom honor is due." All of these phrases are familiar. But how about this one: "Honor yourself." Does that feel right to you? If it doesn't, it's only because you haven't heard it enough to form a habit in your mind and actions.

You may be surprised by just how many people don't have a healthy respect for themselves. When people don't respect themselves, it always shows. It's impossible to hide. One way to determine if people have a healthy respect for themselves is to watch how they keep their word to themselves. If you can't commit to do for *you* what you say you're going to do, then you really don't honor yourself. There are people who give to others but never give to themselves. That is not honoring.

Some people make time for their spouses, their children, their work, their church, and their friends, but they feel guilty about taking time for themselves. They are not honoring themselves. They deserve to treat themselves well. Compassionate samurai will honor themselves, whether it's by having a massage, spending time in the hot tub, or reading. Those behaviors aren't selfish unless it's carried to the extreme of not having time for others. If you don't take care of yourself, you'll eventually become a martyr and not be of much use for anyone else. Service is a bottomless pit. You always want to contribute, but don't fall into the trap of thinking that you can finish or complete your duty.

Do you exercise and eat right? That is a self-honoring practice. What do you say to yourself when you make a mistake? Do you honor yourself by saying that it was a good effort and look for the lesson you learned? Do you dishonor yourself by berating yourself or calling yourself stupid? Samurai honored themselves highly. That is the main reason they felt so compelled to honor other people they came into contact with, even their enemies. How a samurai treated himself was an indication of his overall image.

It is that kind of image that others see in you, and that image you can give to others. How you treat yourself is a direct reflection of how you'll treat others.

The Power of Your Mentor

Vulnerability is more attractive than invincibility. In the army I was taught the opposite concept. I make it a point to talk about my mentor often to show honor. Some people feel strange talking about other people; they have an issue with honor, but it's that they don't honor themselves. Others operate from a mind-set of scarcity and are afraid to give people recognition. Although people act as if they invented this or that item, very few people originate brand-new concepts. We improve on what others have already popularized long before our time. King Solomon was quite right when he said that there is nothing new under the sun.

Every time I mention my mentor, Tom, I actually honor myself and increase the value of my personal worth. People trust me more when I unashamedly identify with another man, letting them know without reservation that he's responsible in large part for the success that I enjoy today. One thing that most achievers have in common is that they all have a mentor whom they credit with their knowledge and success. An average person sees life in terms of independence. That is far different from compassionate samurai, who see life through the eyes of interdependence.

There really is no such thing as independence. Everyone is connected whether we want to acknowledge that truth or not. It's when we realize how powerful our connectedness is that we realize and actualize our collective worth. Without someone to follow, I'm lost. People who are lost cannot make meaningful contributions to the universe. It's important to hook up with someone who can lead you to where you belong—someone who has been there already.

Dishonor Makes You Small

Dishonor diminishes a person's value. Some years ago during a championship fight, Mike Tyson bit Evander Holyfield. It shocked the entire sports world that he would do such an animalistic thing. Tyson was disqualified, fined, and reprimanded by the boxing association. He dishonored himself, and his fans dropped him like a hot potato. The ramifications of his act not only affected him and embarrassed his family, they sullied the boxing profession as well. The whole industry began to look like a joke.

Traditional samurai would kill themselves by seppuku rather than embarrass their family or group. Seppuku was an incredible act of courage, in which they stabbed themselves in the stomach and then made seven sideways strokes. The samurai's body died, but his reputation survived. Mike Tyson was a great fighter, the champion of the world. But in an instant, in the eyes of his worldwide audience, Tyson's action transformed him into something weak. His dishonor made him look small.

There are people who dishonor their family name, particularly in families with long-standing traditions of wealth and contribution. If you belong to a wealthy and respectable bloodline, you have to choose your friends and your dates carefully. You can't hang out with criminals when you have a name and a tradition to uphold. In one sense, it has been more difficult for my children since I founded Klemmer & Associates Leadership Seminars because they haven't been able to act like normal kids. They realized that it could affect the business and the reputation I've spent years building. In another sense, it was good for them.

I think all people should look at themselves as royalty with a name to uphold. In some families it may not be obvious, but it is there nonetheless. At West Point, we learned the values of "Duty, Honor, and Country." These are the core values of the motto. They are the code of a compassionate samurai.

Did you do your duty? It doesn't matter whether you liked it or not. Duty comes first. You honored your country and your military unit as well as yourself by doing your duty. An average person might consider letting himself down, but you couldn't let your unit or country down. The academy had the honor code, which said that cadets couldn't lie, cheat, steal, or tolerate anyone who did. The code required us to turn in anyone who violated any of those codes. The civilian world called this ratting someone out. We believed that following this code honored the overall reputation of all our fellow cadets.

We cared so much about that reputation that we would turn our best friend in. That is the level of commitment to principles that compassionate samurai possess. This value took most of the cadets some time to get into their heads. For example, if you violated a regulation like drinking alcohol on campus and got caught, you received a certain punishment like walking the area and being confined to quarters. If you lied about the fact that you drank, then you were expelled because that action violated the honor code.

No lie was too small—and it only took one time. If you were asked if you'd shined your shoes and you said yes when you hadn't, you were expelled. Outsiders sometimes thought this was too severe, but cadets rarely did. It established an unbelievable context in which to live. In the beginning, many of the cadets adhered to the code out of fear of being expelled. Over time, they moved from compliance to true commitment to the code. Compassionate samurai have the highest standards, and they measure themselves against that standard, not by the standard the world follows.

A Compassionate Samurai's Actions Affect Everybody

It's one thing to dishonor yourself, but you can never do just that. Your actions reflect on all your affiliations: your work group, your faith, your country, and all other compassionate samurai. A samurai's actions are never his own. Compassionate samurai collectively share their actions with everyone else. When a samurai dies, other samurai honor him by bowing before him, even if he's on the enemy's side. If they do not properly honor the opposing samurai, they will die as punishment.

In our modern vernacular, this concept is closest to team loyalty and support. Life is really about being on a *huge* team. Our facilitators all sign an ethics code. If they have sex with a student or use illegal drugs, they will be let go. There are seminar companies and individual speakers who use their platform and position of authority to take advantage of their participants. Life on the road has its temptations. Such acts would not only dishonor them, they would dishonor their families and Klemmer & Associates as well.

You can't win in life in the
most real sense until *everyone* wins.

For most of our team, the threat of dismissal creates compliance to the code, but the desire not to reflect poorly on and disappoint their co-workers who have done incredible things for them creates commitment. It is this realization and experience of duty to the team that upholds their honor. You can't win in life in the most real sense until *everyone* wins. Unfortunately, we've come so far from this concept of win-win, that we've lost the sense of living to help others live and, in the process, gain a profound sense of life.

Average people never care about their actions or whom they affect. They just live each day for their own pleasure, not thinking about the trail of negative seeds they're sowing. Average people don't think about others; they're selfish. Compassionate samurai live their lives for the value, benefit, and reputation of others, for their team as a whole.

Compassionate samurai hold principles above personal benefit. Average people do whatever is best for themselves.

Grad Story

In 2003 Bill Kelly took our seminars. At his peak prior to that year, Bill had made $200,000 a year as a real estate broker and had worked himself ragged to do it. I purchased a fourplex from him in Santa Rosa, California, and complimented him on what appeared to be significant weight loss. He had lost 53 pounds and kept it off for a year. I asked him how he'd done it. He teased me replying, *"If How-To's Were Enough, We Would All Be Skinny, Rich & Happy,* silly." (That's the title of my first bestseller.) He then explained that he'd established the habit of honor after attending our Samurai Camp.

As he learned to respect himself, he began to honor his body. He started working out regularly on the treadmill. He realized that certain foods were hindering his overall health. So he began to choose healthful foods. He no longer reached for potato chips, sodas, and candy as his quick fix but began making sensible choices like vegetables, fruits, and water. He viewed eating bad foods as dishonoring his body.

Instead of seeing working out as drudgery, he looked at it as honoring his body. Needless to say, Bill lost the weight and has maintained his health. He didn't do it by high-impact dieting or overworking himself at the gym. Instead, he chose to see his physical body as a vessel of honor, worthy of the best treatment and the highest-quality foods. It's not that how-to's are bad. It's that by themselves, how-to's are insufficient.

People know how to lose weight: eat less and work out more. Our behavior, however, is driven by beliefs in our heart. Bill's income skyrocketed to over $600,000. People like to be around those who honor themselves. His new lifestyle has attracted clients, and it has affected the type and quality of clients he attracts. And the best news of all is that he's done it by working less and increasing the quality of his marriage and lifestyle. It's an honor approach.

*Compassionate samurai have the capacity
to trust others and themselves with their life
and the wisdom to know when to do so.*

*Average people are either unwilling to
trust others to be as trustworthy
as they are, or they trust blindly
without doing due diligence.*

Chapter Seven

TRUST

> *"You may be deceived if you trust too much, but you*
> *will live in torment if you do not trust enough."*
> — Dr. Frank Crane

One of the most overused and underappreciated phrases is "I love you." These words have so much power, yet when we put them to the test to prove our love, we often fail. The main reason is that we don't think through the impact of this phrase before we say it. Many people use this phrase as a tool to gain access to certain areas in life. Many times, a man has used this phrase to sweep the woman of his dreams off her feet. After he got what he wanted, perhaps he took her for granted or even started treating her poorly—and the relationship was lost.

That, of course, isn't always the case. But why does it happen? It happens because trust was broken. The words *I love you* have the power to gain access, but they do not have the power to keep you at the point of your desire. Trust can maintain a relationship through many difficult challenges, and that's true in business and personal relationships. For the most part, this phrase has lost much of its power because it is used so often without much conviction. That's unfortunate because these words carry a power-packed punch when they're used properly and thoughtfully.

Compassionate samurai have the capacity to trust others and themselves with their lives and the wisdom to know when to do so.

The phrase *I trust you* can carry equal power, if not more, when used appropriately. These three words are very powerful. However, many people are scared to use them; they're unable to trust themselves or others to any large capacity. Some don't even see the benefits of trust. Compassionate samurai have the capacity to trust others and themselves with their lives and the wisdom to know when to do so. If you want to be a compassionate samurai and lead an extraordinary life, then you *must* know how to trust.

Many of us were brought up not to trust. When I was very young, I was taught that I lived in a dog-eat-dog world and that if I didn't look out for myself, no one else would. It is true, in my experience, that much of the world doesn't operate from a position of trust. Does that mean that *you* have to? Do you want to be ordinary or extraordinary? To be extraordinary, you must be able to trust. People whose trust has been seriously abused may find it difficult to try again, but they *can*. Love can overlook many imperfections. Trust does not. Trust demands perfection. Unlike love, trust must be earned.

What is trust? To trust someone is to rely on the character, ability, and word of that person. What do the words *I trust you* mean? If I say "I trust you" to my children, that may mean I trust them to come home by curfew. I trust them not to do illegal drugs. But I don't trust them to make financial decisions for my company. Trust is item-specific. So, *I trust you* is an inaccurate and misleading statement.

Why Trust?

Unless you see the benefits of trusting, you may be tempted to slide through life without trusting. There are five benefits that motivate a compassionate samurai to trust:

1. It's the only way to access the synergistic power of teamwork.
2. It builds relationship and intimacy.
3. It releases time freedom and efficiency.
4. It's the primary tool for making a difference and being of service.
5. It gives you a feeling of exhilaration.

First, let's deal with the synergistic power of teamwork. Synergy is the idea that the whole is greater than the sum of the individual parts. In other words, $1 + 1 = 3$. Suppose you can lift 50 pounds with your left arm and 50 pounds with your right arm. Normal math would indicate that you could lift 100 pounds using both arms. In reality, you end up lifting about 140 pounds. Where does that extra 40 pounds come from? It's a scientific phenomenon known as synergy.

In the financial arena, if three or four people pool their resources—whether it's money, time, or specific investment knowledge—they can get much higher rates of return. With only $10,000 to invest, you have certain opportunities. With $100,000 to invest, many more opportunities are open to you. With $1,000,000 to invest, you have even more to choose from. But in order to pool your resources, you must trust each other. Many people don't want to trust others in that situation, thinking that they'll run off with their resource.

"I wouldn't want to work hard looking for an investment if they aren't working hard." No one wants to be taken advantage of. But if you don't trust, you cannot have a team or synergy. Then you're condemned to being ordinary. You may be a big fish . . . but only in a little pond.

Second, without trust, even if you make it to your desired destination, you'll be alone. You won't have anyone to share your joy of winning.

In the movie *The Godfather*, Al Pacino's character rises to the top position as "Godfather" by trusting certain people. He employs the synergistic power of the team. As the sequels progressed, however, the trust eroded, and eventually he found himself alone. Some businesspeople either step on others to get ahead or they don't share the recognition. Trust is broken. When that happens, they are alone, and no one is eager to help them. Their power is reduced.

This scenario relates to the third benefit: time freedom and efficiency. When people can't trust, they're unable to delegate. Yes, they can do a great job, but now they must do everything. Their ability is limited by the number of hours in a day. By trusting, they can unleash the wondrous power of leverage and get work done, even when they're not working. They can seize opportunities that they would have missed. Huge burdens can be lifted from their shoulders.

I love fund-raising for great causes. If I simply donated my money, I could only give so much. When I ask others to trust me and to trust that they themselves are capable of replacing what they donate, then we can raise exponentially more money than I could ever give alone. It inspires more people to get the job done. We create more together than if we act alone.

In the workplace, if trust is nonexistent, information flow slows to a crawl. It becomes inefficient. In the average working environment, honest feedback is rare because trust has been broken. Perhaps someone trusted a co-worker with sensitive information and it was used against him. Perhaps feedback was given, not with the intention of helping the person, but to make him feel bad about a mistake. Making decisions with insufficient information leads to poor decision making and also creates a hesitancy to make decisions at all.

The fourth benefit is that trust is the primary tool for making a difference or contributing. When you trust people, you empower them. They play at a higher level, trying to live up to the trust you've placed in them. In our process of training facilitators, there is a point when the trainer begins leaving the room for longer and longer periods. Students always comment that the facilitator trainee seems to "magically" transform, becoming almost another person as he lives up to the trust being placed in him. If you want to make a difference, you must learn to empower others by trusting them.

The fifth benefit is that trusting another human being or yourself produces a feeling of exhilaration. It's a high, a rush. There's nothing wrong with that. A compassionate samurai deserves to feel great. Think about a time when you trusted others to do something and they came through. Perhaps it was the first day you let one of your children drive your car without you in it. Maybe it was when you first let your child walk or ride her bike to school on her own. It could have been the time that you bought your first house and trusted yourself enough to pay off the mortgage. Do you remember how your child felt? Do you remember how *you* felt? You were on a high.

So with all these benefits, why aren't more people trusting? It's because trusting carries its own risks. You can be hurt to a greater degree and more quickly when you trust. You lose control when you trust. If I trust you to do a job, you are making the decisions—not me. There are simply different costs and benefits to trusting and not trusting. It's all a matter of what you want to deal with. Compassionate samurai take the maximum gain strategy of trusting whenever possible. The average person plays not to lose by not trusting.

The Risk/Reward Ratio

Some people are the perpetual victims of abuse. This type of individual tends to be a glutton for unnecessary pain, trusting without any sense of knowledge or inner conviction that the person is worthy of trust. I'm sure you know people who constantly give their trust and their heart to others without first putting them through any kind of screening process. Perhaps you've seen people invest large amounts of money in a project, simply because their favorite celebrity has invested as well. They didn't investigate the project or exercise due diligence. This behavior has nothing to do with trust. It's irresponsible. Trust must be earned. It's built by risking increasing amounts of money, time, authority, your feelings, or any other resource.

Compassionate samurai are trusting and they receive trust, but they don't willingly enter into dangerous enterprises expecting to be disappointed. That's not intelligent. Samurai are always ready to give their trust to another person, even a stranger. They won't hold newcomers accountable for a breach of trust if they're innocent. Yet, they don't trust people who haven't proven themselves trustworthy. Years ago, a friend recommended that I invest with Josh Murakami, an investment broker. I didn't invest with Josh simply because my friend did. Yet I see many people invest tens of thousands of dollars on the basis of a recommendation. A compassionate samurai wouldn't do that.

I performed due diligence. What were Josh's credentials? How much money did he manage, for how long, and what were the rates of return? I didn't simply take Josh's word for results; I talked with current and previous investors. You've certainly received investment newsletters that claim to predict the stock market. Just because they make a prediction, you don't have to believe them. Check them out. After my investigation, I decided to invest some money with Josh. Did I invest all my investment capital? No.

I invested $25,000, an amount I could afford to lose. Although I wouldn't have been happy to lose that money, it wouldn't have affected my lifestyle. So, I tested his performance for a year. He returned 50 percent on the money and sent out monthly reports on all the trades. I put more money in. He returned 50 percent again. The third year, the return was a 15 percent gain. Josh had earned more trust by managing the money and giving returns.

In our business, certain employees can't spend money without prior approval. Another level of employee can make a $500 purchase. These employees have shown how they think and what kind of decisions they make. That's why they've been promoted. They earned our trust to spend at that level without checking. A management team member could make a $5,000 decision without checking. They've earned that authority. If they make several poor decisions, however, they'll lose our trust and consequently lose that authority.

The same thinking applies in relationships. Some people make a huge commitment like marriage without exercising due diligence. Again, this is not trust; it's irresponsible. Exercising due diligence means asking tough value questions before you get married. Find out about her past. Get to know his parents. As I write this, my wife, Roma, and I have been married 23 years. I've been on the road giving seminars at least half that time. Because of the due diligence she performed, Roma trusts me. It's been hard, but she made that choice.

Compassionate samurai would never have an affair because it would violate the principle of honor. Taking that path would dishonor my family name, my wife, our company's reputation, and the very name of a samurai. My years of making the right choices have earned my wife's trust, and now she doesn't even give it a thought.

We also need to trust ourselves. What do we trust ourselves to be able to do and not do? I would never bring a woman to my hotel room for a meeting of any kind without at least a couple of men present as well. Even if nothing happened, it would create a problem of perception. And I have everything to lose if I failed in a moment of loneliness and temptation and succumbed to a reward of minimal pleasure.

In business, there's a principle called the risk/reward ratio. It simply means that there's no significance without knowing both the risk and the reward involved. If I told you to put $10,000 up and you had a 90 percent chance of losing it, would you do it? You can't make that decision. It means nothing. If I tell you that you have a 90 percent chance of losing and the return if you win is $1,000,000, now you have a ratio and a significant number. Now you can make a decision. Perhaps you could have a 99 percent chance of winning, but your reward is only a delayer, you have that ratio and can make a decision.

Compassionate samurai consider this ratio in the arena of trust. They have the capacity to trust totally, but they're wise about when and where they place that trust. Do you trust yourself to pick the right person for a serious relationship? Do you trust that if an employee makes a mistake, you can recover? Do you trust yourself to make the right decision? Do you trust that God will really provide for you? You must build up and earn trust in yourself, just as you do with others. When you fail to trust others, it's not always the other people who have the problem or appear to be suspicious.

The samurais' approach to having their trust broken
is to learn from what happened and move on.

Usually inability to trust identifies a much greater problem within you. Often, it means that you're not trustworthy. The other extreme is equally as unfruitful, which is, because of past abuse, you choose to close the door to anybody ever entering your life. I realize this is a self-protection mechanism, but it doesn't work. It's neither valid nor reasonable. Every samurai knows how it feels to be hurt or double-crossed, whether it happened in a business deal, a relationship, or even a close friendship. The samurai's approach is to learn from what happened and move on.

Gone in a Second

True samurai know very well that they'll need the interdependent support of a team to accomplish their life's purpose and mission. If they become paranoid because of a negative situation, they'll never fulfill their goals in life. Early in my company's history, I trained a man to be a facilitator. He was very good. Then I made him a partner, sharing equity in the revenues that were generated. He'd made some poor private financial decisions and became financially challenged. Later he became greedy and tried to steal the business. He didn't succeed. I thought that we'd established a good working relationship and friendship over the years. But in the moment of his greed and his ill-conceived actions, all of the trust that I had for him and in him was suddenly gone. That didn't happen because I thought he was perfect and could do no wrong, but rather because I didn't believe that he would breach our trust over money. I'm not sure that there's ever a legitimate reason to break trust, but a compassionate samurai would certainly never do it over money.

To the compassionate samurai, money is a means of exchange. It's an illusion to which we give a value. From one point of view, it's only as real as we make it out to be. Money is easily replaceable; it's not rare. It doesn't have an intrinsic value. The paper notes can easily be destroyed by fire or water, or even blown away by the wind. To lose a relationship over money would be a reversal of values to a compassionate samurai and not something he would ever do.

The aforementioned man has even asked to work for my company again, but it won't happen. Why? The risk/ reward ratio. There is really little to gain by having him come back, since I can train other great facilitators. There is much to lose, though, in time, energy, heartache, money, and so on. I've forgiven him, and I can honestly say that I love him and wish him well. I just don't trust him with our company's future.

Can a compassionate samurai trust someone else to be a partner? Absolutely, but an average person can't. In fact, several years ago, I trusted two long-term team members, Patrick Dean and Steve Hinton, to become partners. It was necessary to create the synergistic power and leverage. It has paid off handsomely for everyone, and we have touched many more lives than if I'd continued to run the business by myself. Trust can be viewed much like the construction of a skyscraper. It may take several months to draw up the blueprints for the building. To assemble the right crews to do the work could take months. The building itself could take years from start to finish. Yet the right force against the building can take it down in less than an hour. A breach of trust can have such an incredibly strong impact on a relationship that it can destroy it in no time.

A compassionate samurai understands how to gain, manage, and cultivate trust. Perhaps you've heard people say things like "I don't trust anybody anymore." It's easy to see that these people have been badly hurt by broken trust. In reality, they aren't being honest. No matter how much you want to bar yourself from ever trusting anyone again, it's not that easy to accomplish. As long as you live, you have to trust people over and again.

If you believe that you don't trust anyone, then why are you reading this book? You somehow believe that I have something of value to say to you, so you trust me at some level. You trusted whomever you bought this book from. Did they give you back the appropriate change, or did they rob you? It took trust to expect that they'd give you back the proper amount.

Compassionate samurai don't try to escape trusting others; rather, they look for opportunities to extend their trust to others.

Did you purchase this book with a check? If you did, did you make sure that the person who took the check didn't take down your bank's routing number and account number? It's possible that they may be able to tap into your account and withdraw funds from your account. If you gave them a credit card, the person may charge your card to the max. I could go on and on, but I'm sure that you're getting the point. In the most basic sense, we are almost coerced each day into trusting others, from catching a subway or a train, to trusting a fellow driver to stay on his side of the road.

You can't escape giving others your trust. Compassionate samurai don't try to escape trusting others; rather, they look for opportunities to extend their trust to others. Samurai know that their very life is often totally at the mercy of someone whom they've trusted. To withdraw trust is to withdraw life. And to withdraw life prematurely is to abort your mission, something that a samurai never does.

Inspect What You Expect

Here is a gross misconception. People think that if you check on them, you don't trust them. That's untrue. Just because you inspect doesn't mean that you don't trust. It really means that you're being a good steward over your time, your investments, and the people you've been entrusted to care for. Often this scenario occurs between children and their parents. The parent will tell the child to do a particular chore, and when the parent inspects the child's performance, the child screams, "You don't trust me!" It's not that the parent doesn't trust the child; the parent has a responsibility to inspect the situation to ensure that the child has carried through on the task.

The inspection actually increases trust when the job is performed as requested. It provides feedback that helps make course corrections and keeps the child on task. There is an old business adage that you must inspect what you expect. Scuba divers always go with a partner. They check each other's tanks. It's not that they don't trust each other or think the other is incompetent; it's because of the risk involved. There is so much is at stake: a human life. The odds are that we can make a little mistake that costs a huge amount, so it doesn't matter if the odds are only one in a thousand.

Even in a marriage, this concept holds true, although there must be some fine-tuning depending on the marriage and the people involved. If the husband constantly promises to be home at a certain time yet always has an excuse when he *doesn't* show up on time, his wife will no longer trust him—at the very least, she won't trust him to show up on time. But it can bleed into other areas until she wonders what else she can't trust about him. This is why a compassionate samurai would never lie, cheat, or steal.

When trust in your word is broken, nothing else can be trusted. Honesty is the very foundation of trust. During the Cold War, President Reagan supposedly said to Soviet president Gorbachev, "Look, the truth is I don't trust you. You don't trust me. Given that, where do we go from here?" It was that honesty that enabled the two leaders to work together in a spirit of diplomacy that eventually led to the demolition of the Berlin Wall.

Some people carry this idea to an extreme, checking constantly that tasks are being performed. That is inefficient and untrusting. They value control more than increased production. Remember the risk/reward ratio: What is at stake and what has been proven? The more a person has proven to you, the less is at stake and the less you should be checking up on him or her.

Compassionate samurai don't take the issue of trust lightly. They are trustworthy, and they expect others to be trustworthy as well. It's human nature to expect of others what you expect of yourself. If you're honest, you expect others to be honest. If you're a liar and a thief, it would be ridiculous to expect others not to lie or steal from you. We receive in life what we're willing to put out, but that doesn't mean that if you're trustworthy you can trust others.

Trust is something that I expect to receive, so I give it. I expect trust from the people I truly love even more. I give trust because I desire more intimacy. In life, you never get what you want. *You get only what you inspect.* What you're not willing to inspect, don't expect. It's rather interesting that an airplane pilot still uses a checklist despite the fact that he may have flown the same type of aircraft more than a thousand times. Why the need for such a thorough inspection? It should be second nature to fly safely to his destination.

The reason he keeps the checklist isn't because he doesn't trust himself. It's the risk/reward ratio. The pilot has a lot at stake. Ignoring the inspection process could cost innocent lives. It's very likely that if he doesn't go through every single item on the list, the plane will still arrive safely. But suppose one thing was out of order on the checklist? What if there was frost on the engine or a leaky valve? A seemingly minor oversight could cost the lives of many people. It's all about personal and corporate accountability.

Businesses can lose millions, if not billions, of dollars annually if they don't inspect their workers, their management, and their factories. I'm not talking about calling people on the carpet when they've done something wrong. I'm talking about simply comparing what was expected to what was done. Do you know what you expect? Do people know what you expect? Unclear expectations lead to mistrust. Inspecting is done before a project is completed, not after the fact.

I've heard people complain that they don't like a job "where somebody's always looking over my shoulder."

If you ever hear that, watch that person closely. In my experience, people who make comments like that are often sluggards; they are trying to beat the company out of money. It's not a crime to want to work in an environment where you're not constantly monitored. But honestly, you have to earn such a position. You don't become a self-governed person after years of sloppy living.

If you want to get to the top, you *manage* your way to the top. Compassionate samurai are promoted regularly, not through manipulation or coercion, as some people choose. Compassionate samurai advance from level to level, not by inspecting others under their command, but by first inspecting themselves. So you're not ready for a promotion until you've first inspected yourself. And you aren't ready to inspect others until you first inspect yourself. One reason people fail to reach their goals of weight loss, financial independence, or even marital success is because they lack accountability.

Accountability means that you're tracking results. Average people leave those areas to chance, falsely believing that they'll work out in time. You can't expect anything of yourself that you're not willing to inspect. A pilot checks the equipment frequently because then the corrections are small and easy. Small errors that go unnoticed or uninspected for hours can result in the plane's being so far off course that it's too hard to make a correction.

- *Trust*—an equitable right or interest in property distinct from the legal ownership of it: a property interest held by one person for the benefit of another.

According to this definition, a trust is held not for your benefit, but for someone else's. Compassionate samurai live their lives thinking about the benefits of others first. They maintain trust to benefit others, not so people can look at them and applaud them for being so good and trusting. There is so much at stake that other people will need to know that they can invest their trust in you, without having to worry about their decision.

When people have second thoughts about deciding to do business with you, it could be the result of a number of things. It could be buyer's remorse; they simply didn't see the value in parting with their money for your product. It could be that the person isn't trustworthy and tends to distrust everyone else. Or it could be that something about you spelled out distrust to them. Even in business, you must always be more concerned about how the client benefits from the transaction. Once you gain trust, keep it!

A High Price to Pay

The samurai takes the principle of trust to extremes, and rightly so. There is always a high price to pay when trust is at stake. Some years ago I was trying to obtain Chevron Corporation as a client. The deal looked favorable. The final piece to the puzzle was to be determined in a phone meeting that was supposed to take place at a certain time. I was five minutes late for the conversation. Their senior executive told me that if he couldn't trust me to respect his time, he certainly wasn't going to trust me with Chevron's money, and he hung up.

We lost what would have been a very large contract over five minutes. We lost the potential contract because of a loss of trust. I failed to earn his trust. Although I was upset, I understood what had happened and I resolved never to repeat the mistake of overlooking how each decision affects others' trust in me. His actions have helped us make millions of dollars since then. I learned a valuable lesson about trust. You may think, *You didn't even know that guy. How unfair! It was only five minutes.*

This man trusted me to be on time for a phone conversation. He had the power to make important decisions for Chevron, involving large amounts of money and human resources. He must have earned that trust along the way in his career. As a steward of his company's resources, he was demanding that I abide by the legal definition of trust. He had to look out for the better interest of his company by weeding out the symptoms of distrust. The only barometer to measure my trustworthiness was whether I kept my word by calling him when I said I would.

In his mind, I shouldn't have expected a second chance to prove myself at a greater level when I'd failed on such a small level. There are always hidden costs when trust is breached. Remember that. There is a very close relationship between trust and agreement. Broken agreements create broken trust. When you break your agreement with a person, you have created a situation in which that individual may never enter into an agreement with you again.

Dr. Aaron D. Lewis, a spiritual leader and writer, recently told me that he was asked to accompany his spiritual mentor, Archbishop LeRoy Bailey, Jr., to New York City for a meeting with author Bill Hybels. During the meeting, Aaron slipped away to purchase a charger for his phone because his battery was nearly dead. He walked around the corner to the New York Electronics Company to buy the charger, and the clerk told him that the charger was on sale for $69.95, if my friend had the cash.

Dr. Lewis only had about $100 in his wallet and didn't want to spend most of his cash on the charger, not knowing what he might need the remaining cash for later. There was nothing special about the charger. It looked like a regular charger for a cell phone. The clerk began telling my friend that this charger was special because it could fully charge a car battery in under 20 minutes. The information on the package didn't verify what this guy was saying. As my friend was walking out the door, the salesman yelled out that he'd take just $40 in cash for the charger.

Needing the charger, Dr. Lewis gave the man the money and went on his way. Later that day, he stopped by a T-Mobile store to find out what their phone charger should cost. To his surprise, the T-Mobile charger was priced at $19.95. He couldn't trust the salesman in the electronics store. Now you may be wondering, *What does it matter? New York City has so many tourists and millions of potential customers that it really doesn't matter about one person's business. Right?* Wrong.

Compassionate samurai are always concerned about contribution. They are givers, not takers.

Samurai are long-term thinkers. They consider the relationship, not the immediate deal. One of the benefits of trust is relationship. Honor, respect, and trust are long-term values. You can make money selling drugs, but you're not contributing to humanity. Compassionate samurai are always concerned about contribution. They are givers, not takers. In a transaction, they're always more concerned about how they can give to the person with whom they're doing business.

The Value of Relationship

Trust is earned. Some people ask, "How can I trust someone I don't even know?" Well, you don't have to know people in order to trust them. In fact, people are usually taken advantage of more by people they know than by strangers. It starts with a decision. Trust others and you gain relationships. Relationships will carry you through tough times. That's one of the benefits of trust. As you know, tough times will come.

The store manager of the electronics company in New York who intentionally overcharged my friend is probably overcharging other people. The time will come when this company won't have as many customers, and they'll suffer more severely than they have to. When you value relationships, you know that those with whom you're in a relationship will always support you during the tough times.

Joe Girard made it into the *Guinness Book of World Records* for selling more cars than any other salesperson. He accomplished this feat by charging less and doing more

135

volume. He could have tried to charge more from one or two customers, but he would've lost those customers and perhaps many more because they wouldn't have trusted him to give them a good deal. Girard coined the "Law of 250," which says that the average person has a circle of about 250 people he can influence.

So if you give great service, you may increase your business by 250 people. If you offer horrible service, you may decrease your business by 250 clients or sales, or maybe even more than that since bad news tends to travel faster than good news. For example, about 20 years ago, I was in downtown San Francisco and my Jaguar started steaming, so I called AAA's road service. They asked me where I wanted to haul the car. Without thinking, I told the man to haul it to a mechanic I'd been dealing with for years in Marin County.

I didn't even consider the 50 or so mechanics in between San Francisco and Marin because I trusted my mechanic. I know very little about mechanics. On numerous occasions, he could have easily charged me an extra few hundred dollars, but he didn't. If I needed a $6 radiator cap, that's what he sold me. We'd built a relationship of trust over the years. That's why I paid several hundred dollars to tow the car 35 miles instead of going to someone I didn't know two blocks away for free.

One of the industry niches our company serves is network-marketing and home-based businesses. This is an industry that has been known for making exaggerated claims. People make promises about how much money can be made for almost no work. It's a great industry, but like any other business, you have to work. When people make inflated claims, they may enroll more people initially, but they won't be able to maintain a relationship because the trust has been broken.

When you always speak the truth, including the not-so-pleasant aspects, you build a relationship on trust. These teams stay together through thick and thin for very long periods. This also happens on the church speaking circuit. If a big-time preacher or lecturer agrees to talk at a smaller church or venue and later receives an offer from a much larger church, he can be tempted to cancel the smaller church. That has a larger immediate benefit but carries a huge back-end price. Over time, not only will that person lose the trust of the person who invited him, but he won't get as many engagements overall. People talk, and he'll be considered a bad risk.

Does Competency Overrule Trust?

Sometimes people believe that competency overrules trust or that they don't need trust. For example, in the world of sports, we often see favors given to athletes with above-average athletic skills. In college, maybe even in high school, teachers and professors help athletes pass to the next grade level even though they don't have a concrete grasp of the work. They receive these favors because they're skilled on the court or field, but they aren't becoming trustworthy. Some people overlook this, but it won't last forever.

Terrell Owens is a phenomenal athlete, perhaps the most talented wide receiver in the country. He played for the San Francisco 49ers for nearly five years. He missed key meetings, showed up late, and feuded with the coach and other players. Trust eroded, and despite his talent, he was traded to the Baltimore Ravens. A last-minute controversy brought in the NFL Players Union, and Owens ended up with a bigger contract for more money with the Philadelphia Eagles. He played there less than two years before they released him.

Now he's with the Dallas Cowboys, and things are already shaky. He's on the verge of not being wanted by any team. Eventually, regardless of how skilled he is, unless he changes he won't have a place to go. What happens when he's no longer able to play the game because he's too old? Who will share opportunities with him? It may very well be that his riches will evaporate.

Don't mistake what I'm saying. I don't wish him harm . . . or anyone for that matter. I hope he has a wonderfully enjoyable career, and a long-lasting one. I'm simply trying to convey the message that trust isn't something to take lightly because the road back from trust can be a very long, tiresome, and lonely one. Think prevention, and develop trust habits now that will become your character now and forever. Do the little things that build trust and receive huge payoffs down the road.

The Road Back from Breaching Trust

It would be pretty disappointing if we ended this section without offering some hope. If you've been in a situation in which your trust has been compromised and you failed those who trusted you, realize that not everyone is going to extend trust to you again. Some people are going to shut you out for life—that's just the way it is. That's the price you sometimes have to pay.

Others may forgive you and allow you another chance to rebuild a relationship with them, but I can tell you this much: If you choose to burn someone twice in a serious way, you might as well hang it up for life. Your name will become so tarnished after a while that no one will want to deal with you at all. And when that happens, you'll be left in a most vulnerable state. You need the help, assistance, protection, and love of other people. Simply put, you need other people's support. So here are two things that you need to do to rebuild your trust with someone once you've lost it.

1. Start making commitments and keeping them! There is power in commitment. When you make a commitment, you bind yourself to your word. When you keep your commitment, you earn trust. You are no more than your word, so start keeping it. Start small and build up. It's no different from lifting weights. You don't start off lifting 300 pounds. You build up to it. It's the same with trust. Start with small agreements and keep pushing yourself to larger ones.

2. Start making yourself accountable to others. The more authority you have, the easier it is not to hold yourself accountable, especially to people with less authority. I believe that you ought to make yourself accountable to those at both ends of the spectrum. Accountability gives you an ability to have more in your account. It's the only way to have lasting increase in your life, and it's the safest way.

Compassionate samurai have the capacity to trust
others and themselves with their lives, and have
the wisdom to know when to do so.

Compassionate samurai ask, "How can I?"

Average people ask, "Can I?"

Chapter Eight

ABUNDANCE

"You can't afford poverty."
— Unknown

B ooks dealing with prosperity usually don't place chapters on money and abundance first. There's a very good reason for this. Before you can understand abundance, you really need to be prepared. You need a foundation on which to build. Readers tend to skip the other chapters and go straight to the one they believe will release them from their prison of debt and poverty. The truth is that the reason they're in the prison of indebtedness in the first place is because they've approached their lives the same way that they read those books. They skip over everything.

Be Willing to Pay the Price

One of the first components of an abundant mind-set is that you must be willing to pay the price. There is no free lunch. Certainly there are faster and more effective ways to do things, but compassionate samurai are willing to invest time, money, effort, and even failure to create what they want. Average people look for the easy way out. They skip steps. They ignore important information, not realizing that they need to understand it in order to pass to the next level.

You can't skip the basics and expect to move to the intermediate level. It just doesn't work like that. Some people dream of buying hotel buildings, but they don't own a home. It's very difficult to buy a hotel if you've never owned any property. First things must come first. It's not impossible. All things are possible. It's just highly improbable. Look around . . . average people want to achieve great success but they avoid the steps necessary to attain that goal. Owning a multibillion-dollar corporation, for example, is a very lofty goal. But it's attainable.

The average person wants to bypass the years of learning about finance or attending seminars to develop people skills. Managing a smaller business that earns several million dollars a year can teach you the lessons of cash flow and succession planning as well as maintaining the context of a business culture as your number of employees rapidly expands. The point is that abundance doesn't just happen. It occurs in stages. Some of the best training I received as a facilitator was when I volunteered to conduct home-party presentations to market seminars for my mentor, Tom.

It wasn't simply that I learned presentation skills or content. I had to deal with and learn to connect with the most resistant people—people who had never heard of Tom's seminars and who felt as if they'd been forced to listen to the information I was presenting. I learned to deal with the most adverse conditions, like a baby screaming during the middle of my talk, and how to predict and avoid problems ahead of time. I didn't get paid for this, but these are lessons I've applied thousands of times in my career as a facilitator.

There were others who thought volunteering was beneath them or who just didn't want to spend the time. They just wanted to be facilitators. Guess what—they never made it. They wanted to jump to the top rung of the ladder without climbing the bottom rungs. Years ago, I was willing to pay the price to be where I am now.

Twenty years ago, Lance Giroux, a very dear friend, and I, along with our wives, traveled to Hong Kong. At one point during the trip, Lance wanted to exchange some money. There seemed to be money-exchange stores every 50 yards downtown. I recommended that he not exchange any money. When he asked "Why not?" I replied that all the signs said no commission charged, no sales fee. "When something looks like a free lunch and you don't know the price, the real price is usually too high." As an experiment he exchanged $100. He received approximately $84 back. They took 16 percent! They simply called the fee something else. *There's a price for everything.*

Know the price, and based on the reward or benefit, decide if it's worth paying. If it's worth paying the time, money, or energy, then be willing to pay the price.

There's an old adage: "Don't step over a dollar to pick up a dime." That's a waste of time and a way to regress in terms of abundance. The abundant thinker doesn't mind putting out in order to get more back. I've heard people complain about the fees that some financial planners charge. They may charge $4,000 to $5,000 for consultation. Occasionally, someone who hasn't taken our seminars will comment that our seminars or books and CDs are too expensive.

Are the financial planners' fees or our seminars fee too high? The answer depends on the kind of service you receive from your investment. It's one of the reasons we measure results and publish them on our Website. For example, our weekend Personal Mastery seminar costs $500 to $900. Based on the results of our surveys, the average person in a home-based business or direct sales increases his or her income $352 a month after taking our seminar. In a year, that's a return of $4,224 on an investment of $500 to $900.

That's a return of 500 to 1,000 percent. Compassionate samurai don't sit around counting pennies when they could be counting $100 bills. Compassionate samurai are willing to pay for experts—such as financial planners, tax strategists, real estate brokers, nutritionists, health coaches, or relationship experts—who can truly make a difference in all areas of their lives. They pay these experts to be a part of their system and to educate them.

Before abundance manifests in a tangible
way in your life, it must first manifest in your mind.

I've used a financial planner to develop a 412i benefit plan. Without getting too technical, a 412i defined benefit is a pension-plan investment in the stock market. With this plan, the investor doesn't lose when the stock market goes down and gains 60 percent of the increase when the market goes up. I use this plan as a portion of a conservative base to my investment portfolio. During the stock market crashes of 2000 and 2002, it saved me well into six figures. I'd never have even heard about this type of investment if I hadn't been willing to pay the financial planners their well-deserved fee. Average people try to save a few dollars by doing it themselves. Pay the professionals well, and learn enough to ask the right questions.

Before abundance manifests in a tangible way in your life, it must first manifest in your mind. If abundance never takes root there, then you'll probably never experience it. So if you skipped the previous chapters, stop now and start reading this book again from the beginning. Read the Introduction. Do it now! If you've already passed that point, then it's all right for you to pass go. Let's move forward and condition your mind for abundance.

The Scarcity Mind-Set

Let's approach abundance from its opposite aspect: the scarcity mind-set. Scarcity is the position that there's never enough, and it's usually based on the person's assumption that he or she is not enough. The average person looks around and sees nearly 7 billion people on the planet, and thinks, *I'm only one person. I'm not enough.*

Then life experiences validate that feeling. He doesn't do well enough in school. She isn't able to make friends or keep her parents from getting a divorce. Then these people look outside themselves and say:

- There aren't enough customers.

- There aren't enough good men or women.

- There isn't enough time.

- There isn't enough money.

- There isn't enough oil.

- There isn't enough love.

- There isn't enough _____. [You fill in the blank.]

The compassionate samurai realizes that his *wholeness and completeness doesn't depend on external circumstances.* Etch that into your brain. That's our definition of *abundance.* It's a very different definition for abundance than how most people define it. The average person thinks abundance is a certain amount of income or net worth. Some great philosophers like Buckminster Fuller define it as the number of days you can go without working and not decrease your lifestyle. Those are fine definitions, but ours is a fundamentally different approach.

Abundance is the position in which your wholeness and completeness are not dependent on external circumstances.

You receive wholeness and completeness from birth because of your spiritual nature and your connection to God. Since God is infinite, you are complete because you're connected to Him. In addition, your wholeness and completeness depend totally on what is inside you— nothing else. If you don't have anything inside (that is, character), you will always be forced to prove your worth through the attainment of things. That is, in fact, where the average person seeks validation—on the outside through friends, titles, jobs, and material wealth.

Haven't you noticed the number of people who are endlessly accumulating more stuff without ever being happy? When a person tries to use material things to fill that hole of satisfaction, it's never enough. It's no different from an addiction. There are people who drive Rolls-Royces and Bentleys, yet they are poor spiritually, mentally, emotionally, and yes, financially. They continue to rob good ol' Peter and never even pay Paul.

Some live one deal away from foreclosure and repossession. That's a scarcity mind-set. I know people who change cars every year so that their friends, neighbors, and co-workers think they're doing well. That's scarcity thinking. Some people can't keep a stable address. They move from the West Coast to the East Coast, from New England to Florida, and so on. They move almost every year. Not always, but many times, they're looking for something outside themselves to fill a hole of dissatisfaction. They haven't distinguished satisfaction from the "more-better-different" realm.

One of the challenges with the U.S. as a whole is that the average person is looking for satisfaction in the material realm—hence, the feeling of emptiness. Other countries see America's great material wealth and mistakenly link it to spiritual bankruptcy. Compassionate samurai understand where their satisfaction comes from and choose to play the more-better-different game in order to create. But they never look for validation in that realm because it's an endless game. Seeking satisfaction there becomes an addiction.

Another example of the scarcity mind-set is someone who has to work all of the time and can never take a day off. She believes that she can't afford to lose a day's pay and that things can't function without her. That, too, is scarcity thinking. I've seen people who have six-figure incomes, live in palatial homes, and drive luxury cars, yet if their spouse asks them to spend time with the family for a weekend—they can't. They work all of the time, make tons of money, and yet they won't take the time to enjoy it with those they love. In their minds, they believe that if they stop working, everything will stop. That isn't true, but some people believe it anyway.

The scarcity mind-set can manifest in many different ways, and someone can have one with or without money. In order to last, the abundance mind-set must precede the manifestation of prosperity in health, relationships, or finances. Recently on my AOL home page, I read the story of a man who'd won the lottery in 2002. By 2007 he was broke, according to the article. Now before you begin thinking that this man lost about $5 million, think again. He won $315 million in 2002 and five years later has nothing to show for it. You figure that one out. He claims that people stole his money. Even if that were true,

I'm sure you'd agree that $315 million is a whole lot of money to steal.

The real deal here is that this man has a scarcity mentality. If he had an abundance mentality, he would have created more abundance with his fortune. Because his mind wasn't conditioned to handle that much money, he didn't know what to do with it once he received it. That is usually the case with many Power Ball or lottery winners. The subconscious thinking and character must change first.

Your thoughts are invariably what will always create wealth in your life. And, your thoughts will create the right habits that facilitate perpetual wealth.

You've heard the phrase "Money makes money." That's not always true. Abundance thinking creates money. Your thoughts are invariably what will always create wealth in your life. And, your thoughts will create the right habits that facilitate perpetual wealth. It's obvious that this man who won $315 million didn't think like a person who would normally have that kind of money. And because he didn't think like a multimillionaire, the money fell through his hands. His scarcity thoughts reduced his net worth right back to the place where it matched his thoughts. What is your thinking like? Do you have a problem with other people's prosperity? Compassionate samurai are never concerned about what other people have. That concern is another reflection of scarcity thinking.

For Consciousness' Sake

Compassionate samurai learn to conquer the subconscious mind before the circumstance occurs. The average person is always trying to overcome the circumstance. My mentor taught me a major lesson on conquering scarcity thinking during tough financial times. In the late '70s, his seminar company wasn't doing well. In fact, they were in debt. With several hundred thousand dollars in overdue bills, they were losing about $70,000 every month. In the midst of all of this, Tom pulls me aside and says, "We need to buy a new car. I need to make a statement to my subconscious mind that even though we're losing money I'm still powerful enough to turn this thing around." At times, consolidation and cutbacks are necessary, but more often than not, training your mind not to buy into the present reality is far better.

Compassionate samurai anchor their vision and let reality adjust. Average people anchor in reality and let their vision adjust. Your mind only produces on whatever it's focused on. If you focus on your company's debt, then you'll inevitably become more indebted. Beliefs are changed through repetition and emotional involvement. Our owning a new Lincoln Town Car at several hundred dollars a month wouldn't change the circumstance, but it could change how we thought about them.

My first thought was *What will the employees think?* I was asking people to hold their checks, to not cash them immediately. Tom said, "That's why we are not buying a Rolls-Royce. We could. But that's too far outside the zone and we'd get more resistance than I want to handle at the moment." Buying a car while in debt was completely counterintuitive at that time in my life. Tom turned the company around, and years later when it was doing very well, he bought a Rolls-Royce. I still remember the graduates complaining.

After the incident with the Lincoln Town Car, I never begrudged Tom whatever he spent money on because I realized how important it was for him to keep his head straight. We all had jobs because of it. Buying the Lincoln Town Car changed his thinking. It actually forced good times to come into existence. That experience also taught me to consider people's reactions, but never to be victimized by them.

Now this won't work for everybody. Why? Because we all respond to stimuli differently. This is *very* important. Some people buy expensive things and incur huge debts, thinking it's wealth consciousness. That's not true. Tom responded to having a Lincoln Town Car by thinking of himself as wealthy. It was what he needed to work on at that time. He was already tithing.

When I made the commitment to tithe, we had to sell one of our two nice cars and buy an old green station wagon for $600. No longer having car payments allowed us to tithe. Other people who worked with my mentor accused me of lacking wealth consciousness, but my understanding of Tom and of abundance was that tithing was a fundamental principle.

Later on, long after Tom died, the company was in very uncertain times. Many of us didn't know if we would have a job. I didn't know if I wanted to stay, and I had no idea what I'd do if I left. Finances were challenging, so as a result of my lesson with Tom and the Town Car, I went out and bought a very nice used Jaguar SJS. At that point in my life, I was tithing, and it was a different issue I wanted to work on at the subconscious level. I was affirming that I was capable of making life work no matter what the circumstance. There are times when what you do may not seem too reasonable to the people watching you. Compassionate samurai don't worry about that. They live by their principles.

Tithing, the Practice of Abundance

Tithing is the practice of giving away the first tenth of your income to wherever you receive your spiritual guidance. Typically, this is your church, temple, or synagogue. For the moment, put aside the spiritual aspect and let's look at this from an abundance perspective. How do you change belief systems? By repetition and emotional involvement. The more emotion is involved, the fewer repetitions are needed. The less emotion is involved, the more repetitions are required.

Average people suffer from a scarcity mind-set, and the consequent behavior is to hold on to whatever they hold sacred: money, time, or possessions. Imagine that every time you receive a check you give 10 percent to your church, synagogue, or temple. Can you feel the conflict a person with a scarcity mind-set would go through? That's emotional involvement. How often do you receive income checks? Weekly, bimonthly, monthly? That's repetition.

Perhaps you know people who tithe and who aren't well off. I wondered the same thing, especially after tithing worked so well in my life. That's because there are other principles involved. In the Old Testament, a prophet named Malachi (3:10) said, "Bring all the tithes into the storehouse that there may be food in my house, and prove me now in this, says the Lord of hosts, If I will not open for you the windows of heaven and pour out for you such blessing that there will not be room enough to receive it." If you want to do your own research, it's an easy one to find, as it is the last book in the Old Testament.

Another principle or character trait already covered in this book was *personal responsibility*. Tithing puts us in a position to be blessed, but we're all still responsible for doing our part and walking through the door. Some people tithe and think money will just drop on their head. Tithing is the beginning–it's a great way to combat scarcity thinking.

From a spiritual perspective, you tithe to wherever you receive your spiritual nourishment because it's a way of acknowledging God as the source. Giving to good causes such as the Cancer Society or Girl Scouts is an offering beyond tithing. From a strictly financial perspective, every act of giving, no matter where it's given, combats scarcity thinking.

Receiving, the Hidden Obstacle to Abundance

One of the keys to abundance is your ability to receive. The average person doesn't have the capacity to receive abundance. How could that be a problem? Receiving is easy, you think? Not so. Imagine you have a water glass and someone starts pouring the ocean into it. Would it matter that the whole ocean was being poured into your glass?

You can only keep what the glass will hold. The average person needs to increase the size of his or her glass.

Once, a pastor asked me to coach him in finances. I asked him if he tithed. He chuckled and said, "Of course." I knew him to be a giver, but it can be surprising who doesn't tithe. Then I asked if he invested 10 percent in himself. His eyebrows furrowed, and he asked for further clarification. "Do you take the second tenth of what you earn and invest it in stocks, real estate, or something that is for the sole purpose of increasing your net worth?" He said he'd never been able to do that.

He gave to his church, to his children, to friends, to strangers, but he never gave to himself. He hadn't worked on his ability to receive. When you give to yourself, you're changing what your subconscious says about you. It starts saying you're wealthier. It says you're worthy. If you believe you're born in God's image, then you're a king. Compassionate samurai are able to receive because they feel worthy. Average people don't feel worthy to receive.

When I bought my first Jaguar, I felt embarrassed to drive it. My feeling of unworthiness was fighting me. Compliment the average person and he says, "It was nothing. "A compassionate samurai says, "Thank you." Give an average person something and she will reply, "I can't take that."

Humility is understanding that God is the Source, not you.

Average people confuse humility, which is a good thing, with a poor self-image. Humility is understanding that God is the Source, not you. He's the ocean, and He has infinite water to pour into you. You're worthy of the finer things in life. Make a practice of spending time and money on yourself. It's not selfish as long as you balance it with giving.

Getting a System in Place

This is why, in the financial realm, the system of 10-10-80 works so well. Compassionate samurai give the first tenth to the place of their spiritual nourishment, the second tenth they invest, and the remaining 80 percent they use to pay all the expenses, including taxes, groceries, car payments, and other donations. Compassionate samurai make sure to increase the first two categories as they grow, always keeping the giving and investing at the same percentage. Thus, they're continually better off living on a smaller and smaller percentage.

This systematic practice of giving and receiving (investing) activates the power of compounding interest. Most people are familiar with the principle, and yet few implement it. Investing $100 a month at 16 percent interest accumulates to more than $3 million dollars in 40 years. Average people are myopic. They only see the immediate impact. They think that $100 won't change anything. Perhaps they look a year out and think that $1,200 won't change anything. The average person doesn't see that the power of compounding interest can create $3 million.

The same is true with time. If you write for 30 minutes, five days a week, you could be an accomplished author in less than six months. It just takes discipline. Systems leverage your time, money, and abilities. Systems are tools that create abundance. You have to have a system in place if you want to live in abundance. First of all, abundance is not so much something that you live in, as it is a principle you live by. If you live by the principle of abundance, you will experience abundance.

There are things that you have to do, and they must become part of your character if you're going to be abundant. The traditional samurai was always frugal, not cheap. Frugality, or valuing the worth of things, is a wonderful system to live by. It will always ensure that you're not overspending or being unnecessarily wasteful. Having a budget or a plan for how you allocate your income is a system. Average people either don't have a system or they don't follow it. Compassionate samurai have a budget—no matter how much money they earn. It's a way of thinking.

The system operates like a flight path to determine where you return. Systems don't box you in; they create flexibility. For example, at Klemmer & Associates, if an employee is going on a trip and the flight hasn't been booked four weeks before the departure date, our system sends the person a reminder e-mail so we can get the best fares. In our busy world, it would be easy to book at the last minute from time to time. That little system saves us (conservatively) more than $25,000 a year. What systems can you put in place to enhance your life?

Being Solution Oriented

One of the keys to abundance is having a solution-oriented mind-set. The average person thinks of himself as positive, but he's not solution oriented. As I was writing this chapter, a moderately successful interior decorator came to our house. We started talking about what I do for a living. I gave her some books, and she was very excited. I mentioned a seminar we were holding locally in a few weeks. Instantly she said, "I'd like to, but I can't because I work Saturdays." She had an average mind-set, not the mentality of a compassionate samurai.

When average people ask themselves, "Can I do this?" they base it on the circumstances they see. This woman thought about her schedule, and when she asked the question "Can I?" she came up negative. *An abundant thinker asks different questions.* An abundant thinker asks, "*How* can I?" This simple twist of semantics changes everything. It forces your mind to create a solution. If this woman had asked herself, "How could I attend?" her subconscious would've begun searching for an answer.

In our Personal Mastery seminar, we do an exercise in which everyone crosses the room using a different mechanism. One walks. Perhaps the next crawls; the next person dances across. Eventually, someone gets stuck and doesn't know what to do. We never force anyone to do anything, but amazingly, things usually start to happen. When you say, "I don't know what to do," you're saying that your conscious mind doesn't know what to do. That's the smallest part of you. Yet average people are victims to their conscious mind. That's all they are aware of. Your subconscious can solve hundreds of problems that your conscious mind can't.

A compassionate samurai isn't reasonable. Average people are reasonable. Reason resides in the conscious mind and has a very important function, but it's not to solve problems. Reason looks at circumstances and at your past. But all that your past tells is what beliefs you operated from. The past has nothing to do with what was possible because you can change your beliefs. The conscious mind is the smallest part of you. At this point in the exercise, everyone is usually cheering for the person who was stuck. Our facilitator will pull a $100 bill out of her wallet and give the person 30 seconds from when she stops talking to come up with a unique way across the room.

Within seconds, an idea will hit and the person will get across the room. There are many points to this exercise, but the one to focus on right now is "How many ways are there to cross a room?" There's an infinite number. There's always a way. Average people, however, employ scarcity thinking and believe that there's only one way to do anything—one way to buy a house, one way to sell a house, one way to get promoted, one way to talk with your children. The average person is worried about finding the one way.

Quit worrying about it. The next time you're stuck, remember this exercise and think like a compassionate samurai. There are an infinite number of ways—even when they're not visible. A solution might involve people you don't know but have access to. The solution might involve money that either isn't in your possession or that you can't see. A solution might involve knowledge you don't have and can't see. Compassionate samurai force themselves to look for a solution by asking, "How can I?"

Super-Size That, Please

If there's always a solution, how big are you willing to think? Average people think small. Average people think about what their eyes and ears tell them. Compassionate samurai just naturally super-size it and ask, "How can I increase this ten times?" I once had a conversation with Tom Schreiter, who is an icon in the home-based business industry, a best-selling author, a giver, and a multimillionaire. I asked, "Tom, you are a best-selling author, and I, too, have a best-selling book called *If How-To's Were Enough, We Would All Be Skinny, Rich & Happy.* What would you do with my book?"

He replied, "How many do you sell at the back-of-the-room sales?"

"Typically, a few hundred," I answered.

He said, "Start thinking about selling 10,000 in a sale instead."

I asked, "How would I sell 10,000 at a time?"

He answered, "Start with me," and we cranked out a deal on the spot. Within two months, I made two more 10,000-book sales with other people! I started looking at selling them by the box to achievers, so I started making a lot of 100-book sales. The possibilities were there all along. I just wasn't thinking big enough.

My friend Bob Harrison, who is a real live compassionate samurai, is called Dr. Increase because of who he is and what he attracts through his teaching. He bought a mansion for a dollar and no monthly payments. It's more complicated than that, but it's true. Check out his Website (**www.increase.org**); you can find out the whole story. It started with an ad he read that said: "No reasonable offer refused." He thought, *If they won't refuse a reasonable offer, maybe they won't refuse an unreasonable offer!*

He was thinking much bigger than his finances at the time. Average people don't go looking for huge deals or even allow themselves to dream of the possibilities. What would it be like for you to earn twice what you're currently earning? What would it be like for you to raise a million dollars for a cause you believe in? What would it be like for you to have a job you were twice as excited about going to each morning? Can you take a current dream and double it? Can you multiply that by ten?

Yo-yo Thoughts of the Average

We've talked extensively about the scarcity thinking that afflicts the average person. Some people are so imbedded in it that they live in poverty, whether times are good or bad. There are others—compassionate samurai— who live in abundance no matter what. In fact, frequently, more millionaires are made during economic depressions than during economic booms. The majority of people, however, ride a yo-yo with their prosperity and in all areas of their life.

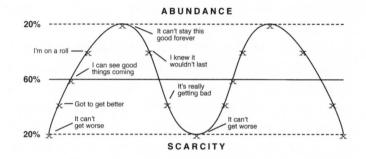

ABUNDANCE

20% — It can't stay this good forever

I'm on a roll

I can see good things coming

I knew it wouldn't last

60%

It's really getting bad

Got to get better

It can't get worse

It can't get worse

20%

SCARCITY

Start anywhere on the graph. Average people think, *It's got to get better.* It gets slightly better. Then they think, *See, I knew it would get better.* It gets better. Then they think, *Good times are just ahead.* Then, *I can't imagine it getting any better.* That's when their success starts to level off. They start thinking, *Good things don't last forever. All good things must come to an end.* And their results start to slip. *I knew it couldn't go on like this forever.* It starts getting worse. *Oh, this is bad.* It keeps getting worse. *This is terrible. It can't get any worse.* They bottom out. That's when they think, *It can't stay this way forever. It has got to get better.* And the climb starts all over again.

There is no lack. There is more than enough.
You are more than enough. Thus, there is an
abundant supply of everything you need!

The truly abundant mind-set is never swayed by the economy, recessions, or even inflation. The abundant mind-set is always well grounded in the reality that if abundance does not seem to exist, then I'll have to create it. They realize that the universe has more than enough resources to go around, enough to make everybody happy and full. So there's never a reason to be covetous or envious of another person. If you can't handle other people having great amounts of money without feeling jealous, then you have a scarcity mentality.

There is no lack. There is more than enough. You are more than enough. Thus, there's an abundant supply of everything you need! As a compassionate samurai, you must build a character of abundance. It must live deep inside you so that you don't have to think. Whether circumstances are good or bad, whether you're riding high or low, you think abundance.

Take life on. Look for challenging problems to solve. Sooner or later the challenges will squeeze you—and that's when all these character traits, including abundance, will emerge. When you squeeze an orange, juice comes out because that's what is inside the fruit. When life squeezes you, greatness will come out.

℃℃

Compassionate samurai ask, "What will happen if I don't take this risk?"

Average people ask, "What will happen if I fail?"

Chapter Nine

BOLDNESS

*"One isn't necessarily born with courage, but one is born
with potential. Without courage, we cannot practice any
other virtue with consistency. We can't be kind,
true, merciful, generous, or honest."*
— Maya Angelou

What comes to mind when you think of courage? A small child may immediately think of a lion as a symbol of strength, courage, and gallantry since many were taught that the lion is the king of the jungle. Even in *The Wonderful Wizard of Oz*, the famous children's book written by L. Frank Baum in 1900 and brought to the screen by MGM in 1939, the lion is missing the quality that should most define him: courage. As the movie unfolds, he discovers he always had it—he just didn't show it.

Fear had so crippled the lion's ability to see himself as he actually was that he lived as a frightened coward, rather than the brave beast that all animals feared. We assume that lions are supposed to be dauntless, no matter what the obstacles are. *The Lion King*—the third highest-grossing animated feature film ever released in the United States, and one of the most prolific and successful Broadway shows ever—depicts Mufasa, king of the pride's lands, and his progeny Simba, the young heir to the throne.

Mufasa was a courageous lion, a protector of his family and land. However, his boldness and courage were not easily transferred to Simba because he was still learning the truth about courage. After each lesson, Simba's uncle Scar would immediately seek to undo everything that Mufasa had taught the young lion by instilling fear in him. Perhaps you haven't realized that you, too, are a lion, at least symbolically speaking. You have the courage, but are you displaying it?

Are you more like Mufasa or the Simba we see at the beginning of the movie? Average people don't take risks, and they know it. They choose comfort and security over opportunity. The average person is in a job she doesn't like, and she stays there because she thinks she has to—she's afraid to change. The average person is afraid to address certain topics in his relationship. The average person goes to church but won't voice her questions and doubts because she's afraid of being judged and ostracized.

The average person in business is afraid to give up any control and is trying to do it all by himself. He's like the lion in *The Wizard of Oz,* trembling and searching to find the courage he thinks he has lost. *The good news is that you have it!* Just like the Oz lion or Simba, you already have courage—but don't celebrate just yet. You, too, will have challenges that you must face *so that you can display courage.*

As those lions did, you will have to come face-to-face with some hard-hitting realities about yourself. First, you are a warrior and your are being is called to win major battles in life. However, adversities and obstacles are bound to occur. When that happens, how will you respond? Will you run for cover, or will you run toward danger, knowing that you have the innate ability to overcome any obstruction that may come your way?

For the compassionate samurai, courage isn't something they display every now and then, but rather something that they showcase every moment of their lives.

Compassionate samurai eat problems for breakfast, lunch, and supper. They do it for fun. They see it as part of who they are. They look at every problem as a set of weights that will help them grow stronger. For the compassionate samurai, courage isn't something they display every now and then, but rather something that they showcase every moment of their lives.

Danger Is Your Opportunity to Awaken Courage

Most people have experienced various events throughout their lives that have convinced them that they don't have courage. Courage sleeps quietly until it's awakened by an opportunity to confront danger head-on. Compassionate samurai look for danger as an opportunity to awaken their courage. Several years ago there was a beautiful statue of Buddha in the middle of a town in Thailand. To accommodate construction, it had to be moved. The statue turned out to be much heavier than anyone had anticipated. When workmen attached chains to the statue and to a vehicle and attempted to drag the statue, the pressure cracked the exterior of the Buddha.

Underneath was a solid gold Buddha that had been plastered over and then nicely painted. It had sat in the center of the town for several hundred years and no one had known how truly valuable it was. Apparently, centuries earlier, the village had been under attack from a warring tribe. The townspeople wanted to protect their gold statue but couldn't move it before their enemies invaded. Their solution was to cover the gold with plaster and paint—and it worked!

That's much like you and me. Sometimes we haven't acted as lions. We've allowed events to bury the real us. Some people become so covered that they forget they were ever lions, much less that they should possess courage. The key to revealing the gold statue inside the plaster Buddha was the applied pressure of the chains when the people tried to move it. Compassionate samurai see pressure as an opportunity to see the beauty inside and awaken the sleeping character of courage.

Low Self-Esteem and Courage

Sometimes low self-esteem is connected to a lack of courage. We fail in business, we fail in school, we're turned down for a date, or we overeat and see ourselves as weak.

The list goes on and on. Our interpretation of events claims that we lack courage (read the chapter "Facts Are Meaningless" in my book *When Good Intentions Run Smack into Reality*). If low self-esteem is directly correlated to a lack of goodly courage, then having courage is the recognition of your potential. It's when you discover your potential and worth in life that you're able to confront every enemy seeking to dissuade you from tapping into that potential. People who don't realize their potential are typically bound by fear—fear of the unknown. That fear usually handicaps their ability to fight forward, leaving them in a worthless position. Let's look at the definition of *courage* in *Webster's Dictionary:*

- *Courage*—the attitude of facing and dealing with anything recognized as dangerous, difficult, or painful, instead of withdrawing from it; quality of being fearless or brave; valor.

Courage is the attitude of confronting danger or even your greatest fear. Look at the famous biblical story of David and Goliath. I'm not convinced that David was born with the courage to fight a giant whom all his predecessors feared. In fact, many translations of the Bible say that when Goliath appeared, everyone ran. Everyone would include David, wouldn't it? It would include the king. It would even include the men chosen to be on the front row for that day. Imagine that. Here are veteran soldiers trained and prepared to die, and they were afraid!

Courage is not the absence of fear. To do something when you're oblivious to the risks involved isn't courage.

Courage is acting in the face of fear. It's looking fear in the eye and spitting in its face. If you have fear, welcome to the human race. The minute you care, there's fear. That's okay. It's natural. It's a scary world to raise children in, no matter what kind of neighborhood you live in. With about 50 percent of marriages ending in divorce, marriage is a frightening venture, too.

With the majority of all businesses failing, it's unnerving to start your own business. Growing old with diminished physical capacity is scary. If you're not afraid, you're smoking dope. In fact, if you choose liquor or drugs, you're still afraid, you've just covered up those feelings. What comes next is courage. Courage is a response to fear. David was afraid, but eventually he stood up to Goliath. What helped him display his courage?

1. David practiced courage before he got to Goliath.

2. David kept rewards in front of his face.

3. David used a support group.

4. David capitalized on his strengths rather than copy someone else's.

5. David used his connection to an infinite God to overshadow the fear of his eyes and ears.

Regardless of your faith, this is a great story to learn from. Take the time to read it in I Samuel 17.

1. Practice.

David combatted his low self-esteem with practice. He was a shepherd boy. How many times have we asked ourselves, *Who am I to do this?* David kills a bear and a lion before he kills Goliath. He worked his way up in courage. Sometimes people try to skip rungs on the ladder and reach right for the top. If you own a home but you don't have an investment property, don't take every penny of your equity and roll it on your first deal. Kill a bear first. Take a portion of your equity and do a small deal. Then try a medium deal. Eventually you may build up your courage and be able to roll it all on a spectacular opportunity.

If you're widowed or simply haven't dated in years, killing a bear might not even be going on a date, but simply going out with a group of mixed singles. The heroic firefighters who climbed the stairs in the collapsing World Trade Center during the tragedy of September 11, 2001, had practiced entering buildings on fire many times. They saw it as simply doing their job. If there's a fear that's preventing you from moving on with what really matters to you in life, practice confronting it. Don't confront it foolishly; approach it systematically with a goodly demeanor.

Even failure requires courage. Just look at what Michael Jordan, a clutch basketball player, has to say:

> I have missed more than 9,000 shots in my career. I have lost almost 300 games. On 26 occasions, I have been entrusted to take the game-winning shot and missed. I've failed over and over and over again in my life. And that is why I succeed.

We live in a society that looks down on and condemns the person who fails. What people fail to realize is that no one ever becomes a success in life without having first had multiple failures. Simply because you've failed at something doesn't mean you're a failure. Would anyone call Michael Jordan a failure? Thomas Edison had many failures before he made his light bulb work, and he had significantly more failures after he pioneered that great invention. Colonel Sanders, the famous founder of Kentucky Fried Chicken, lost dozens of jobs before he started KFC and created a multimillion-dollar success.

Compassionate samurai practice climbing out on the limb until it breaks. Then they dust themselves off and do it again.

My mentor called me into his office a few weeks after I'd started working for him. He asked me, "What has been your biggest failure here in the first few weeks?" I thought for a moment that maybe I'd done something wrong. Then, since nothing had come to mind, I proudly stated that I hadn't made any mistakes.

He said, "Oh. We have a serious problem. You need to know that I've never fired anyone for making a mistake, even someone who made a $100,000 failure. But I have fired people for not risking. If you haven't failed, then you must not have risked enough. Your assignment is to make the biggest failure you can in the next two weeks."

I was shocked. My whole life had been spent avoiding failure. He wasn't telling me to fail on purpose. He was telling me to risk until I failed.

All the fruit of life is out on the limb of the tree while the average person clings to the trunk. Compassionate samurai practice climbing out on the limb until it breaks. Then they dust themselves off and do it again. They become professional limb walkers. Practice! Become numb or neutral to failure. Courage is a maximum-gain strategy.

2. Rewards Are Okay.

In the story of David and Goliath, David asked what the reward would be for killing Goliath. He was promised tax freedom for life (his descendants, too) and the king's beautiful daughter in marriage. David kept these benefits before him as a mechanism to eliminate his fear and help him act with courage. It has been said that fear is an acronym for False Evidence Appearing Real. When you continually repeat and rehearse rewards, the reward in your subconscious mind will banish the illusion of fear. Compassionate samurai display courage simply because that is who they are, but you can increase the display of courage by creating very tangible rewards.

3. Use a Support Group.

Remember, all good is attacked. Don't resist it—it's the way the world is. Learn to display more courage than any attack can handle. Support can help you do that. Don't go it alone. In a fight between a lion and a tiger, the tiger usually wins because they are fiercer and more courageous. They will do anything to win. However, if there are five tigers versus five lions, the lions will always win because they work as a pack and tigers work as individuals.

You are a lion. Build a team. David's family ridiculed him for hanging out with the soldiers. He combatted their negativity by "turning from them to another." Perhaps "another" meant God or perhaps "another" meant another human being. The Bible doesn't say. For sure, whomever he turned to was supportive. When confronted by fear and negativity, compassionate samurai look for people who will affirm their greatness and the fact that they can fearlessly move forward. After my mentor died, his wife took over and the company changed.

I hung on for many years, trying to change her and the company. I was afraid to leave because I'd never done anything except be in the army and work for Tom. I didn't see myself as an entrepreneur. I had three children, a wife, and about $7,000 a month in bills. I was afraid to go out on my own. As the years passed, the integrity of the company deteriorated. Finally, my wife asked me, "What's the worst that can happen if you go out on your own?"

I replied that we could lose our house, our car, not be able to pay our bills. She told me, "It will be okay. If that happens, I won't like it, but we'll just buy another house and another car. I want you to go on your own. You were meant to do this."

That support gave me the courage I needed. I walked out with no business plan, and I took no one with me. I started in a different arena with corporations instead of public seminars, and we made money—and a difference—from day one. That was 11 years ago. If you don't have that family support, work on creating it at home and actively create it elsewhere. Sometimes in network marketing and other businesses, spouses only notice that they see their mate less often than before. No wonder they aren't supportive. A compassionate samurai is a giver. Give your spouse what he or she wants and you'll get support. Go to meetings, and meet other successful samurai like yourself. Make friends. Help them. Create your own pride of lions.

4. Leverage Your Strengths.

In the story, David tries on the king's armor. It doesn't fit because he's small. He's only 16 years old. So, David goes back to what he's good at: slingshots. Even though this was an unconventional weapon, he chose it to focus on his strength. That, in turn, increased his courage. In guerrilla wars, the guerrilla forces have the strength of mobility and speed. They capitalize on these strengths and avoid fixed confrontations that rely on size and equipment and that they would certainly lose. Business is the same way.

What is your strength in business? Is it knowledge? Organizational skills? Creativity? Drive? How can you capitalize and leverage that strength? This doesn't mean that you should pretend you have no weaknesses. On the contrary, you must know yourself and your weaknesses—and you must find a way to become invulnerable to these weaknesses. What is your strength as a spouse or parent? How can you leverage that? That will give you confidence and courage.

5. If God Is for You, Who Can Be Against You?

Put aside your religious beliefs or doctrine for the moment. In the story, Goliath, a skillfully trained, professional fighter, comes at David. Goliath had the better equipment: a spear and a shield. He was physically superior in size and strength. David's only defense was God. But that is enough. If God is infinite, regardless of your faith, what could stand up to that? You have a conscious mind and a subconscious mind and you're connected to God through your spirit. In a three-part snowman, God is the biggest snowball, the one at the bottom that acts as the foundation.

Having *infinite* on your side is a definite confidence
booster that allows you to display more courage.

Is it possible to be financially successful without God? Yes. Your subconscious is very powerful. But why would you cut off the largest part of you? It doesn't make sense. You are a spiritual being who has a body. Compassionate samurai explore their spiritual nature. They're comfortable with that part of themselves, and they look to that part for guidance. Having *infinite* on your side is a definite confidence booster that allows you to display more courage. You can take on anything, and a compassionate samurai does.

Everybody has viewpoints or ways of looking at things. For years we've referred to these viewpoints as sunglasses. People have many different views about nearly everything in life. You have a pair of sunglasses about maintaining a healthy weight, having lots of money, relationships, children, getting a quality education, job stability, owning a business, taking vacations, and flying airplanes. People only make radical changes when they perceive that the benefits of the changes are more rewarding than the cost if everything remains the same.

Positive change will never occur unless the person realizes that change requires boldness. It really takes courage to make a change in your life, especially when you've been a certain way for so long. I got married in my 30s. Up until that point, I really wasn't involved in many serious relationships with women—I mean, relationships in which I felt there was a potential for marriage. That was the furthest thing from my mind. I had sunglasses around marriage.

For a compassionate samurai, *courage isn't optional.*

One of the reasons why traditional samurai appeared to be so fearless is that they played life as if they were already dead. This isn't a perspective of gloom and doom—it's actually very liberating. A person who has nothing to lose isn't afraid of losing. They play full-out, with abandon. If you started a business and you weren't afraid of losing it, you'd go for broke (hence, the saying). This way of thinking frees you up to play full-out in life. The same is true for a marriage or any project.

For a compassionate samurai, *courage isn't optional.* "No courage" is an option, but not having courage is a price compassionate samurai are unwilling to pay. The body is alive—the spirit is dead. When you don't operate in courage, a piece of you dies. Every action that you take that lacks courage is like cutting yourself with a knife. You end up as a 45-year-old zombie. Just discovering this little piece of information will probably make you far more eager to continue reading to discover why you really don't have a choice in the matter—if you want to lead a meaningful life.

Succinctly put, you have to display courage. And if you're lacking in that area, do whatever it takes to get courage quickly! Average people generally tend to move forward in life when all of the conditions are optimal for them to go ahead. The problem with that mind-set is that conditions are usually never conducive for going forward. What if Mother Teresa had waited for the conditions in Calcutta, India, to improve before she decided to minister to the needs of the poor and needy souls in that region? She would have never started her ministry.

The greatest rewards are typically preceded by some of the greatest challenges. You don't conquer valuable land filled with treasures without a fight, without bloodshed. It's at the point of discovering the *cost factor* when most people tend to run for cover, trying to hide from the only thing that will free them from the bondage of mediocrity. You don't want to do it because you're afraid. Average people are so focused on the cost that they can't see the reward.

I've met many people who didn't want to get married because they were afraid to commit to a lifetime of being faithful to the love of their lives. I know smart, talented men and women who are broke, yet they have all of the know-how to run a successful corporation. They remain unsatisfied simply because they're afraid. They think, *What if she's not the one?* Or they wonder, *What if the business fails? What if I go bankrupt? Suppose nobody wants the services I'm offering?* Or they ask, "How can I know this is the right thing to do?" These are all the average questions of the mediocre person. The compassionate samurai asks, "What will happen if I don't take the bold steps?"

It really doesn't matter what the scenario is, whether it's your timidity about purchasing a piece of real estate, buying a new car, getting married, going into business, joining the church, taking on a board position, or even investing in the stock market. When you choose not to do what you set out to do, it's because you fail to see that you have the courage to move forward past all of the stuff that you've made up in your own mind. The cure: *Do it afraid!* You have to learn to do what you have to do, even if you're afraid. Fear in and of itself isn't your problem. Your problem is not facing your fears head-on.

Just Before Your Greatest Breakthrough

Have you ever heard Chuck Yeager's story of breaking the sound barrier? It illustrates this point eloquently. Yeager is a member of the National Speakers Association. In his talks, he freely admits that he had fear. A U.S. Air Force test pilot, Yeager was the first person to fly faster than the speed of sound. He operated with great courage. All of the pilots who'd tried to break the sound barrier knew that they could die during acceleration if they weren't able to control the plane as it began to shake violently, unaccustomed to such enormous speeds.

If Yeager hadn't pushed himself past the fear of dying, he would never have broken the sound barrier. For compassionate samurai, life isn't about getting comfortable where they are right now. Average people have retirement and a comfortable life as their goal. For a compassionate samurai, life is all about breaking barriers and going to the next level. Once you display the courage to arrive at that next level, you'll have to pack up and move again. Courage has many addresses. It's a continuous journey that requires you to stay in motion.

Yeager knew two men who had flown the same type of plane he was about to fly and had died during their attempts to break the sound barrier. As these men accelerated, their planes had shaken more and more violently. Believing that they couldn't fly any faster, both men had tried to slow down and crashed. Yeager had the same experience. The faster he flew, the more the plane shook. The only difference was that he thought, *If I'm going to die, I'm going to die in style.* He tried to speed up instead of slow down.

Boom! He'd broken the sound barrier and his plane almost instantly stopped vibrating.

Almost always, right before you break through to a new level, your plane or your body is going to shake violently. Think back to when you bought your first house. Your hand was probably shaking a little as you signed the papers for that large loan. Afterward, though, you started to relax. Think back to when you were first dating. You were getting the courage to ask the person out and maybe your lips quivered a bit. After she said yes, you were amazed it was so easy and wondered why you hadn't asked sooner. Courage is spitting in the face of your fear by taking action. Compassionate samurai understand this principle and aren't fooled into backing down as life becomes turbulent and their fear increases. It's a natural part of the order of things and separates the average person from the extraordinary results of a compassionate samurai.

When you're scared and you want to back down, that is exactly the time you should go faster, move forward, and do more. People who are afraid tend to slow down, feeling as if they can't do what they set out to do, so they retract. In the midst of your fear, you must find a way to gain an inner incentive, to go faster than you ever have. My friend Aaron D. Lewis likes to say, "Fear runs much faster than courage, yet it never has enough energy to finish the race."

The Many Faces of Courage

"Courage is the determination not to be overwhelmed by any object, that power of the mind capable of sloughing off the thingification of the past."
— Martin Luther King, Jr.

Courage comes in many different packages and has various faces. One is my father. He wasn't an entrepreneur or a best-selling author. Nonetheless, he's a great man who has displayed a great amount of courage. Toward the end of my mother's life, my father took care of her for nearly two years. She had become ill to the point where she had to be taken care of much like an infant. My dad changed her diapers, cleaned her, and stood by her until she died. At some point, it may have been right to take her to a convalescent home, but she didn't want that. So, my father did what he had to do to make it work. He had the courage to face a daily grind.

Actor Michael J. Fox, who is battling the slow loss of control of his body due to Parkinson's disease, has been an inspiration to millions. Other people face a momentary event such as 9/11, when they either display courage or they don't. No matter who you are, you can display courage in some way because it is in you.

Courage does not always have to be loud and obvious. What is easy for one person to do can terrify another, and vice versa. One person can undertake physical challenges with ease and yet be terrified to become vulnerable in a relationship. Another finds it easy to share his feelings, but he's afraid to start his own business or take on a high-pressure job. Everyone has fears, including those who are afraid to admit it. Your fear is your fear. Don't try to make sense out of it, or compare yourself to anyone else.

How to Win at the Game of Life

Being reasonable and logical often causes us to lose courage. Most Americans educate their children to become survival oriented, not recognizing that this process causes them to die. Average people worry more about their kids' emotional and mental states; they don't want them to be hurt. They overprotect them. Then the child begins to believe that she should play not to lose, instead of playing full-out. She beings to think, *I just want to make sure that I don't lose my job.* Or he thinks, *I'll be open with you if I can be guaranteed that you won't hurt me.*

You can't win at the game of life trying to shelter yourself from every single hurt that may come your way. Some parents advise their adult children not to enter into a potentially wildly profitable business venture, but to stay on their job for the sake of insurance benefits and a pension that they'll receive in 30 years. Winning at the game of life requires courage to do it, without knowing all of the facts. You have to make decisions from your gut. Trust yourself, and trust that God is leading you exactly where you need to go.

You do have what it takes. The person who tries and keeps on trying will eventually get to where she's going. That person will become a compassionate samurai. The person who sits back and does nothing will always live at the lowest point in life—mediocrity. Mr. and Mrs. Average can be defined as the best of the worst and the worst of the best. It takes great courage to admit failure, and try all over again. The lessons you learn from failure allow you to take a different path.

A Word of Caution

Sometimes what looks like courage is actually an act to cover up cowardice or insecurity. My friend Azim Khamisa's son Tariq delivered pizzas to earn money for college. One night, a gang accosted Tariq, and he refused to give up the pizza. The gang leader told a 14-year-old member to shoot and kill Tariq. Perhaps it seems as if it took courage for that child to shoot Tariq. In reality, he was more afraid of the gang leader and being rejected by his peers than he was of being in prison. The courageous act would have been to refuse and stand up to the peer pressure.

Many acts are committed in the name of courage that are, in fact, not courageous at all. Look not only at the act, but also at what is driving the behavior. Azim acted like a compassionate samurai. He publicly forgave the 14-year-old boy, and then he reached out to the boy's guardian and grandfather, acknowledging the shared pain of losing family members. Together, they formed a foundation to stop kids from killing kids. That was a magnificent display of courage. Check out the Website at: **www.tkf.org**.

∞∞

*Compassionate samurai are
satisfied without being settled.*

*Average people are settled
without being satisfied.*

Chapter Ten

KNOWLEDGE

> *"Shall I tell you a secret of a true scholar? It is this:*
> *every man I meet is my master in some point*
> *and in that I learn from him."*
> — Ralph Waldo Emerson

What comes to mind when you think about a person who's knowledgeable? The average person immediately thinks about book smarts, high grade-point averages, Harvard and Yale, or graduating at the top of the class. Others may think about people who work in specialized vocations, such as scientists at NASA who can figure out how to make space travel possible or surgeons who can separate conjoined twins.

The tenth character trait of a compassionate samurai is so much more. This trait encompasses specific knowledge, but it's also about a constant eagerness to learn and the practical wisdom of applying knowledge to a situation to produce a desired outcome. Compassionate samurai realize that specialized knowledge can provide an edge. They're constantly seeking knowledge as well as experts to teach them about topics ranging from technology and finance, to relationships, personal growth, health, and leadership.

Don't Settle for What You Have

Average people are either arrogant and believe they don't need to learn, or they're complacent and think that learning really isn't necessary. As I travel around the world, I've run across thousands of people who don't see the need to attend one of our Personal Mastery or other leadership seminars (see **www.Klemmer.com**) because they think they're fine. In reality, they're asking the wrong question. They *are* fine, but what are they settling for? Do you have to be broke to want more money? Do you have to have a marriage on the edge of divorce to want to make it better?

Let me ask you a question: Do dogs like bones? Most times when I ask an audience that question, they respond, "Of course they do." But they don't. Dogs like steak; they just settle for bones. Think about it. If dogs were setting the table, who do you think would get the bones? I think they would give us the bones and keep the steak for themselves, don't you? What happens is that we feed the dogs bones, bones, bones—until they start thinking they like them.

Dogs start settling for bones instead of steak. It's not that they dislike bones or that bones are bad, it's that they're *settling* for bones. Take someone who'as been in a good marriage for 15 years—a good marriage, not a bad one. What they experience year after year is a good marriage, a good marriage, and more good marriage. It's relatively easy then to start settling for a good marriage instead of trying to create a spectacular one (the steak).

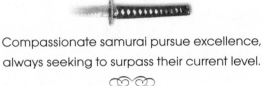

Compassionate samurai pursue excellence,
always seeking to surpass their current level.

I am *not* talking about changing who you're with. I'm talking about making the relationship you're in better. If you have a home, a job, and a nice car, and you make a salary that is equal to or slightly better than most of your neighbors, it's relatively easy to start settling for a good income instead of creating a spectacular income. Compassionate samurai pursue excellence, always seeking to surpass their current level.

Being Satisfied Without Settling

Part of the challenge is that average people get confused and think, *If I want more, I must be dissatisfied with what I have.* Not only is this untrue, but it also creates a box in which being motivated equates to being dissatisfied. Think about the insanity of that. It actually ties happiness to dissatisfaction. Talk about a rat stuck in a maze.

Average people think a *thing* will make them happy. They strive for that thing only to achieve it and find that happiness isn't there either. The problem is that

189

satisfaction doesn't reside in the same realm as *more* and *better*. This is a deep issue that most people must experience to fully understand.

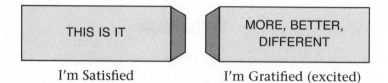

I'm Satisfied   I'm Gratified (excited)

Let's define the terms we're using in this graphic. In the left-hand box, *satisfaction* is the feeling of being in alignment with your purpose. "This is it, and I'm satisfied." In the right-hand box, however, *gratification* is the feeling of achieving something. "I'm gratified by getting more of something, something better, or something different than what I already have."

Think of something in your life you don't like. Perhaps you're in a boring marriage. Perhaps you don't find your job economically or financially rewarding. Maybe you're overweight. Or you may have a serious or chronic illness such as cancer. Pick the thing you don't like and say to yourself, *My marriage is boring and I'm satisfied*. Or, *I'm overweight and I'm satisfied*. If you're an ordinary person, you almost get sick to your stomach saying this. You think, *I can't say that. It's not true*. But you can say it, and *you must!*

You resist making these statements because somewhere deep inside, you think your resistance will change things. It won't. *Your resistance not only won't change anything, it prevents you from creating what you want*. Nonresistance doesn't mean giving up or resigning yourself to something.

For example, in martial arts, you don't resist a punch being thrown at you. The punch simply *is*. You adjust and flow with it, and then you're able to turn your opponent and gain control.

When you resist, you lose control. You lose your ability to create, which is in the more-better-different realm. Think of satisfaction as acknowledging something for how it is (the punch) with zero resistance. *Satisfaction or contentment is found in being where you're supposed to be.* It's found when you're in alignment with your purpose. This requires (1) knowing your purpose and (2) understanding that there are an infinite number of mechanisms for any one intention.

Can you find a way to use the situation of being over-weight to support your purpose? Suppose your purpose was to make a difference or to be a friend, could you use the circumstance of being overweight to help you relate to more people? You could make a difference and have more friends. So from that angle, you'd be incredibly satisfied. You'll lose weight not to feel satisfied because you already are. Losing weight will produce a feeling of gratification and achievement. Do you understand the difference?

This mind-set allows compassionate samurai to be satisfied or content whether or not the situation is one they like. What incredible liberty. Average people resist situations they don't like because their scarcity mind-set makes them think that they can only achieve their purpose through a limited number of circumstances. Put this feeling, which we're calling satisfaction or contentment, over in the box on the left.

Now let's talk about the box called *more, better,* and *different*. Have you ever gotten a new car? How did you feel? It was a rush. Let's call that gratification. How long did it last? It probably lasted less than a few months. You may even have experienced frustration that the feeling didn't last. Within a year, you go out and buy a new car because you want to feel that rush again. We create serious problems when we confuse gratification with satisfaction and contentment.

When you're in alignment with your purpose, things don't matter unless they support that purpose.

Average people seek satisfaction from losing weight, getting a new car, or earning more money. When they don't get experience satisfaction, they fall into depression. They confuse gratification, which is a feeling of achievement, with being in alignment with purpose. When you're in alignment with your purpose, things don't matter unless they support your purpose.

Gratification and satisfaction are in different realms or boxes. This is another topic you can spend years trying to understand, so don't be concerned if you don't get this at first. As always, experiential learning is the best way to grasp this in your heart, instead of in your head. When they first start exploring this subject, some people ask, "If satisfaction isn't dependent on anything being different, why should I even bother with more-better-different?" That's a good question. The more-better-different box is about creation. It creates momentum, and a temporary excitement that we call gratification.

In business, marriage, and health, compassionate samurai create a game of more-better-different for the purpose of creating. The challenge is to operate from both boxes simultaneously, instead of from a place of scarcity in either box. The left box involves being in the moment while the right box lies in the future, creating new possibilities. Playing in both boxes is where you're most effective. Think of great athletes. Usually they love the practice of the sport as much as the game. Masters love to practice until practice becomes a habit.

A football superstar like Jerry Rice is usually the first person on the practice field and the last one to leave. He loves the practice. This is why compassionate samurai "practice," or make daily habits of, the ten traits. Think of athletes when they talk about being "in the zone." They're totally in the moment (left box); they're masters of adjusting to any circumstance and producing what seem like miraculous results in our eyes. At the same time, they're in a game of more-better. The more-better isn't just about the other player or team; they're always striving for better *steak* (remember the dogs and bones).

Average people try to fill the satisfaction box with more-better-different. It can't be done. That's why some people who have money, fame, and material success are still very unhappy or unsatisfied. They're unfulfilled. Average people haven't oriented their circumstances to their purpose; they've gotten lost on the more-better-different side. If you push satisfaction or contentment into the right box, you've built a context or system in which you must always be unhappy to be motivated! Think about that as a box to live in. Remember this: To have proper balance in life, both boxes must always work simultaneously to produce contentment and gratification.

Having a Beginner's Mind

To excel at the more-better-different side is to excel at creation. To do this and be a compassionate samurai requires having a beginner's mind. That doesn't mean that you're perpetually learning the same thing over and over. Repeating the same lesson is not having a beginner's mind. Repeating the same lesson over and over is more like insanity.

> *"Insanity: doing the same thing over and*
> *again and expecting different results."*
> — Albert Einstein

There's nothing wrong with failure. In fact, compassionate samurai don't resist their failures; instead, they use them to draw closer to their purpose. They learn a lesson. Average people resist their failures and miss the lesson. For example, if an average person misses a golf shot, in resisting his "failure," he'll tie his emotions and concentration to the past and probably miss the next shot. Compassionate samurai release themselves from the failure, learn a lesson, and immediately create a spectacular shot. When you fail to recognize why you've failed, you find yourself repeating your failure.

The beginner's mind says, "I've always got more to learn." It's a place of humility. No matter how much I know, there's always more to learn. Say it now, out loud, *"I've always got more to learn."* Saying that will either make you feel great or not-so-great. If you feel not-so-great, it may be because you're dealing with a little bout of pride that makes you think you already know enough and there's really no need to learn anything more. This story will help illustrate this point.

One day a young encyclopedia salesman knocked on the door of a potential customer. After two or three minutes, an elderly man in his 80s opened the door and asked what the young man wanted. The salesman told him that he was selling encyclopedia sets with additional books on the best climates in America. "If you purchase the set, you'll get the additional books as a free gift."

Wasting no time, the old man told the young man, "No need taking out any of those books. At my age, there's nothing more for me to learn. I've been around this mountain a few times and I've just about seen it all. Besides that I've got a breathing condition that acts up in the cold weather here in New England, causing me shortness of breath. Other than that, I'm all right. I suppose I've just got to live with the breathing problem since this here region ain't getting any warmer till summertime." With that, he told the young man good-bye, wished him luck, and closed the door.

Little did this old man know that more than a dozen elderly men and women suffering from the same condition were presented with this offer, bought the books, read the free-offer book on the best climates in America, located the city of their preference for their condition, moved away, and enjoyed another 25 years. The old man who refused the offer died the same month.

The other octogenarians saw this young salesperson as having something they needed, regardless of his age. They still wanted to learn. They had beginner's minds. If learning more meant that they needed to learn from someone who was a quarter of their age, that was just fine. The old man died for the same reason most people die: He stopped learning. You can die physically or you can die emotionally, spiritually, and mentally.

Here is the epitaph for the average man or woman: *John Average Man. Born 1900. Died 1940. Buried 1983.* His body hangs around but he's dead. In countless businesses and homes, you've seen these 50-year-old zombies who have no passion, who have quit living, who merely exist. Some are even proud of it; they'll tell you they're survivors. Compassionate samurai thrive; they don't simply survive.

Unlike the average person, compassionate samurai are dedicated to always learning more because they realize that there's always more to learn. I've heard that the average person reads less than one self-improvement book a year after graduating from school. This is a mediocre mind-set. These people think, *I had enough reading in school. I'm not reading anymore unless I have to.* Compassionate samurai have a voracious appetite to read educational books, listen to learning CDs, and attend seminars.

When you have a beginner's mind, your age is irrelevant, as is your position in a company. A beginner's mind functions at a high level of maturity. At this level, you're not worried about your image. The compassionate samurai's only worry is how to get better. You're open about where you need to improve. But you're blind to your weak spots, if you don't have a beginner's mind. It's not so easy to have a beginner's mind-set in the area of your so-called expertise. The average person wants to believe that he cannot learn anything more in his area of expertise in order to appease his ego. Compassionate samurai care more about learning than they do about ego.

A beginner's mind doesn't mean you don't know anything. But, despite that knowledge, you're going to approach the subject with brand-new eyes. For example, if you've been a manager for ten years, you may lack a beginner's mind. That will make you become obsolete. It's dangerous not to stay a beginner. When you think you know it all, you cut yourself off from your source, because you force yourself to stay in the conscious mind where knowledge resides. Whatever you conceive God to be is not even the beginning of God. You limit God.

Success is a good thing. But sometimes with success comes faulty attitudes and ways. Success can make you cocky. When that happens, you'll inevitably begin to falter because you won't find value in listening to others, especially to those you feel are beneath you. Having the knowledge of a compassionate samurai requires great humility. Remember, compassionate samurai always seek to learn more because they know there's always more to learn. And learning can come in various ways—from people who may be in a subordinate position, from people who are not as smart as we are, or even from strangers.

Aikido demonstrates this principle probably better than any other sport. No belts are worn in a dojo where aikido is practiced. There is a specific reason for this. Titles from outside the dojo mean nothing. Years of experience in practicing the art mean nothing. This practice supports humility. Everyone is at the same level. In Japan, there are no belts—that's an American thing. The Japanese people don't measure progress in the same way Americans do. Not wearing belts and trying to determine rank avoids comparison, and avoiding comparison forces you to look at a person for who they are.

You will be far more open to a person's instruction or advice if you think that they have something relevant to say to you. When you're totally enamored with yourself, it's very difficult to receive from others, even if their instruction is life changing. You have to proceed humbly in this process. Sometimes pastors who lead huge churches with 10,000 members tend not to listen to pastors who have smaller congregations. What a grave mistake! Maybe the pastor of the smaller church hasn't reached the capacity of leading 10,000 people, and maybe that's not his calling.

Be humble enough to receive instruction from those you may not have formerly wanted to receive from.

But he still may have some very significant knowledge to share with his fellow ministers. He may have experiences in ministry that outweigh having a huge congregation. Pride may cause one pastor to shut the other out, thinking that he is not on his level. This behavior occurs in all professions. Be humble enough to receive instruction from those you may not have formerly wanted to receive from.

The Archenemy of Knowledge Is Low Self-Esteem

A huge nemesis to a beginner's mind is low self-esteem. Elaborating on this subject could take an entire chapter, perhaps even a whole book. Low self-esteem can be a problem by itself. But the connection between low self-esteem and a person who refuses to receive knowledge is pretty interesting. People who have low self-esteem try to disguise it in many ways. Some buy extremely expensive clothing to dress up their feelings about themselves. Others try to assume know-it-all image to conceal the deeper problem lurking within. When a person doesn't have a beginner's mind-set, it's often associated with a psychological problem about how they feel.

Right/Wrong Paradigm

Closely associated with the resistance to receiving knowledge with a beginner's mind is the right/wrong paradigm. A compassionate samurai lives outside of right and wrong as an experience. This is very different from morality. The compassionate samurai has a high moral code, as we've discussed. Conduct is gauged against this code, and it is either right or wrong in terms of the code. What we are talking about here is right and wrong *as an experience.*

If they are in circumstances of poverty, they don't make that wrong; they simply apply the code to those circumstances. If they are in a conflict, they don't make being in the battle wrong; they simply apply these character traits or code to the battle. If they're single, they don't make being single wrong, they apply the code to being single. In this manner, they don't resist wherever they are, so all their energy is available to them.

In aikido, if someone throws a punch at you, you don't respond that it isn't fair. You simply say, "Oh, this is how we respond to a punch." If a kick is delivered, it's simply a kick, and this is the way to respond. Average people make many circumstances wrong and resist them. They don't accept these circumstances as being the way that it is and then consume most of their energy in resistance, leaving little opportunity to create. Compassionate samurai don't look at their viewpoint as right and the other person's viewpoint as wrong. That would be like standing on the wet, green side of a mountain and talking to someone on the dry, barren side of the same mountain, and arguing who's right. The compassionate samurai hears the other viewpoint, but he has no need to defend *his* viewpoint. He doesn't judge the other viewpoint. He simply takes it in and looks for its usefulness or relevance to his situation.

That's why compassionate samurai are great at receiving feedback. Suppose a child says to her parent, "Daddy, you don't love me." A compassionate samurai doesn't argue. He thinks, *That's an interesting viewpoint. Why would she say that? What am I doing or projecting that she would say that? Do I need to change how I am expressing my love so that it is heard and not confused with something else?*

The same occurs in business, marriage, and any other arena. Average people argue for their "right" viewpoint, and their situation never changes.

Watch Out for These Dangers

There are some dangers to not being open to knowledge and not having a beginner's mind. Beware of these things and maintain the stance that you're committed to growth and development in every area of your life. Be committed to growing in knowledge, wisdom, and understanding.

1. We will be blind to the lesson that is available to us when we believe we know it already. Don't be a know-it-all. When we think we know everything, we lose out on knowledge.

2. When we're not open to growth and having a beginner's mind-set, we tend to alienate people. When we don't want knowledge, people shy away from us and are reluctant to offer their viewpoint.

3. Life replicates itself. After a while, the same people we mentor begin to think that they know more than us. They close themselves off from what we have to offer.

4. When we think we know it, we become casual and drift off purpose. This reduces our effectiveness in the face of challenges.

5. We lose passion and the freshness of life.

Specialized Knowledge

With a beginner's mind and an eagerness to learn, we acquire specialized knowledge. Have you ever heard the phrase *If only I knew then what I know now?* It's often used to explain a mistake or behavior that looks foolish in the light of new information. When the decision was being made, without the benefit of this knowledge, it didn't appear to be foolish. However, the increased knowledge gives the decision maker an edge.

When I first began my company, I sold a piece of real estate and needlessly paid $60,000 in extra taxes. I just didn't know that I could've saved money on the deal. There were people around who could've counseled me, but I didn't seek them out because I didn't have a compassionate samurai mind-set. As a result, I lost a lot of money paying capital-gains tax on the sale of the property.

My tax accountant suggested that, since I had to pay sooner or later, I should pay right away. I thought all accountants were the same. Accountants all have the rules, but they do not have the same skill levels. Heeding his advice, I wrote the check immediately. About a year later, I began a search for a new accountant, interviewing several who worked for wealthy friends. To my complete surprise, I discovered that there were several legal ways to have avoided paying that capital-gains tax.

That was a hard way to learn that not all accountants are the same. They have different areas of expertise and different levels of creativity. Had I had a beginner's mind-set, I would've been eager to learn about taxes—not to become my own bookkeeper—but to understand why

I was doing what I was doing. I could have questioned others about their experiences to see if I was getting a deal or simply allowing my money to be taken. I strongly advocate paying money to professionals.

Average people, because of their scarcity mentality, won't pay for experts. They will do the work themselves or hire the cheapest vendor. In their mind, it's too expensive. Compassionate samurai are happy to pay top dollar for an expert. They just make sure they're getting expert advice and not simply being overcharged. If I did my taxes, it would take longer, I would miss opportunities to save money, and I would lose the opportunity to make money while I was doing the taxes. I know what I'm best at.

Having a beginner's mind doesn't mean that you've got to do it yourself. It means that you need to seek out knowledge beyond your current level so that you can properly use other people's expertise. If you have a bookkeeper or an accountant, you should still have a working knowledge of where your money is going and how it's being spent. Seeking that basic knowledge is having a beginner's mind-set because you're tapping into resources around you. The samurai connects knowledge to winning.

There are really two different areas of knowledge: specific knowledge and paradigm shifts or revelations. Specific knowledge keeps you on the cutting edge of areas such as finance, relationships, health, and spirituality. Let's look at finance for a moment. What can you learn about earning money? What can you learn about saving money by understanding the tax game? What can you learn about protecting your money? Have you explored the best way to leverage your giving? Yes, you want to hire experts to help you.

If you aren't in that profession, there's no way to keep up with the latest information, but if you don't educate yourself, you won't know the questions to ask to find a qualified adviser, much less to design exactly what it is you want. When was the last time you read a book on relationships? Are you entering a phase of your life with new challenges such as parenting, or an empty nest, or taking care of your aging parents? How much new information do you think has been discovered in the past ten years alone? What are the experts saying about vitamins?

Do you even know what normal cholesterol levels are? What about blood pressure? The amazing thing is how little time it takes. If you spent a half hour a day, five days a week, reading, in five years, you'd become one of the most knowledgeable people in any area. Yes, it requires discipline. Compassionate samurai are disciplined. Begin now. Set a time and a place for regular reading. Not everyone has the same schedules or rhythms.

My wife gets up every morning around 5:30 and reads for at least an hour. It fits her lifestyle, and I've heard many speakers say that this is the way you should start your day. I've never been able to do that. I'm more like a train. I'm slow to get moving in the morning, but once I'm rolling, I go for a long time. My preference is to read at night. If my wife tries to read at night, she only makes it through a page or two. Patrick Dean, an executive in our company who currently heads up our facilitators, reads during the day. It fits his style and daily schedule.

So, find your time and find your place—but read consistently. Don't use your lifestyle as an excuse for not having a system. Now, figure out a system for topics. Do you want to focus on one area for a year? Perhaps you want to choose a different topic every month. Pick your books now. Be a good steward of your time by consciously planning your educational reading time. This doesn't mean that this is the only time you'll read. But there *is* an old adage that says "If you don't plan, then you are planning for failure."

What about listening to CDs or cassettes? Some people just aren't into reading. Maybe you can download your teaching material onto an MP3 player or a DJ Ditty. People have kidded me for years about all the tapes I always have in my car. When I drive to and from the airport, which I do regularly, or around town on errands, I listen to material. Obviously, I can't take notes as I can when I'm sitting at home, but it still leverages my time. Part of my physical workout at home is to ride a stationary bike for 30 minutes and to do stretching, sit-ups, and push-ups. That's another great time to listen to educational CDs.

So far, we've been talking about specialized knowledge. Now let's turn to the second type of knowledge: paradigm shifts or revelations in your belief systems. This kind of knowledge can only be accomplished through experiential learning. That means you're participating in an activity in which you have an experience that changes your viewpoint on something. Are you going to wait for life to hand you the experience you need to enhance your career, relationships, health, or spirituality?

Life is usually the most expensive teacher in terms of time, money, and relationships. That's why I advocate experiential workshops. It's the fastest, cheapest, and most enjoyable way to accelerate your growth. The opportunity to meet quality people who have like-minded values alone is worth the time and money you spend. Some of the paradigms or beliefs that made me successful in the army didn't make me successful as an entrepreneur. That doesn't make the old beliefs wrong. I simply had the incorrect map or paradigm for the new territory or life situation.

Not all of the paradigms that made me successful as an entrepreneur will work to take a multimillion-dollar company to one worth $100 million. It's an ongoing process of discovery. That's why I encourage people to take a seminar at least *every six months. Every quarter is even more appropriate for most people.* That's a beginner's mind-set; that's what a compassionate samurai does. Average people attend one seminar, think they're all the same, and quit.

Think of yourself as your own company, *You Inc.,* even if you work for someone else. If you work for someone else, that job is your main income stream, but you are still your own business. Good business owners will tell you they have a budget for developing their people. Organizational constraint theory basically says the size and effectiveness of any organization is gauged by two factors: its systems and its people. So take a percentage of your gross income and budget it for your personal growth. It's the smart thing to do.

Take at least 5 percent and invest it in your development. If you make $50,000 a year, then spend $2,500 annually on books, tapes, and seminars. If you can, stretch to spend more, just as a fast-growth company invests more. Generally, the more expensive the seminar is, the more successfully financial the participants are—these people make great friends.

Tapping into Resources Around You

Compassionate samurai always realize the potential in others because their strength can be a huge benefit. Compassionate samurai understand that others can help them overcome tough situations. Samurai seek out the most unexpected and overlooked sources. Some of the greatest knowledge that you can tap into exists right in your circle of influence. You really don't have to travel far to receive knowledge, especially if you're really open to receiving. Far too often, however, the knowledge that's right at your fingertips goes unnoticed. It's when you reject that kind of knowledge that you find yourself either repeating a lesson one too many times or missing out on a big opportunity all together.

Some of the greatest knowledge that you can
tap into exists right in your circle of influence.

My wife, Roma, gives me input on various matters, from spirituality to business. Sometimes, I tend to discount her advice, particularly when it comes to business matters, since she's not running a business of her own. That's not what she wants to do. Her heart and her talent lie in her art and her painting. Strangely enough, her feedback is usually directly on target—and if I reject it, I'm rejecting assistance that I may desperately need. What you need may be around you, but it may remain unnoticed because it's not packaged in something you can readily identify. Roma doesn't have to be a business expert to offer her valuable knowledge to me. Sometimes a person who isn't directly connected to your business or vocation can give great advice on a particular subject.

It's an unbiased observation. Businesspeople think business. Athletes think in terms of sports. Preachers think in term of evangelization. Educators think in terms of teaching others and seeking funding to do so in the most efficient manner. There is a great benefit to networking with people who think as you do. There is an equally great benefit in talking to people who have a totally different perspective.

Insight and Foresight

Even having specialized knowledge isn t enough. You may know people who excelled in high school or college and yet can't seem to make ends meet. They can't even land a descent job. How is it that a person can have great book knowledge but cannot accomplish objectives in the real world? Many people have knowledge, but they just can't connect it to their particular circumstances. Others have acquired information that isn't applicable to their lives. Yet other people don't have the courage to apply the knowledge they have.

Statistics show that most people who take real estate and stock seminars never make a deal. Compassionate samurai have the appropriate knowledge, the insight to see its application in their lives, and the courage to apply it. Insight is the ability to see past what your eyes see. The average person sees a house for sale and knows the asking price and the condition of the house. That's what they can see with their eyes. A person with insight sees that, but she also creates significance from how it relates to other information.

Insight leads to foresight, which is the ability to see how things will develop before it happens. Knowledge and experience increase insight. After engaging in numerous stock or real estate deals, a person can develop insight that enables him to look at a property or stock and know he can make money. His conscious and subconscious are in harmony, and he is able to access more than his normal five senses.

The Oarsman and the Adviser

Once upon a time in the days of sailing ships, kings, and queens, there were two men. They grew up on the same street and attended the same schools. They dated some of the same girls and went to the same social functions. One day, they moved apart, but after many years, they ended up working on the same ship. One was an oarsman, and the other was the king's adviser. The oarsman was jealous of the adviser's good job and believed that he, too, should be an adviser. He had the same education, so why not? It just didn't seem fair.

The king overheard his complaints. So when the ship reached land, he said to the oarsman, "Go to the top of the hill and tell me what you see." The oarsman ran up the hill, looked around, came back down, and said that cats were fighting. The king asked, "How many cats?" After climbing the hill again, the oarsman said there were five cats. "What color are the cats?" asked the king. The oarsman climbed the hill again and upon returning, he said there were two black cats and three brown ones. "What type of cats are they?" After climbing the hill once again, the oarsman said they were Manx cats.

The king called the adviser over and said, "Go to the top of the hill and tell me what you see." Upon returning, the adviser said, "There are five Manx cats fighting. Two are black and three are brown. A fellow over the hill owns them. He says that if the cats are bothering you, he will put them inside. However, if you're inquiring because you admire them, he'll give you one." Are you an oarsman or an adviser?

An oarsman does what he's told. He does a good job, but he only does his job. Compassionate samurai advisers look at the big picture, and in addition to doing their job, they ask questions they think their boss might want or need to have answered. Regardless of your job or position, you can be either an oarsman or an adviser. Organizations excel when they have many advisers. I look forward to crossing paths in our journey together as compassionate samurai and in sharing the battles and contributions you've made.

⤳⤲

*Compassionate samurai say what
they mean and do what they say.
They make bold promises and keep them.*

*Average people do what they say
as long as it is convenient.*

Chapter Eleven

FINISHING STRONG

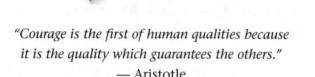

*"Courage is the first of human qualities because
it is the quality which guarantees the others."*
— Aristotle

Congratulations! You have successfully made it through the ten traits of a compassionate samurai. I'm even more convinced now that you have what it takes to carry on the samurai's honorable tradition of displaying integrity and ethics while being bold and courageous in business affairs and in life. One thing that I haven't mentioned is that compassionate samurai always finish what they begin. View what you've learned so far as a start, one that you must finish. You have the tools—the ammunition, if you will—to go into the marketplace and wage a great war.

Don't delude yourself into believing that this is not a war. It's a war of culture. It's a war that pits greed against compassion for all. It's a war that pits deceit against honesty. It's a war that pits domination of others against respect for all. It's a war between the personal comfort of apathy and the courage to care. It's already being fought in the media, in the entertainment world, in politics, in education, and in homes just like yours.

It's time for you to take on mastery of these ten traits and to be a beacon to your world with a backbone of boldness and an intensity of integrity that's an inspiration to those around you. You're not alone. There are thousands of us around the globe in every culture and in every nation, but we are in the minority. It's time to rise up against the selfish pursuit of the masses. It's time to rise above the normality of mediocrity. Let's not compare our success to that of others.

Let's not compare our nation to other nations. Rather, let's train a new generation of compassionate samurai. Let it be said and written in the history books that in the beginning of the 21st century, there arose a people who were not of the same country, or of same color skin, or of the same religion. But these people had the same values and character—and they had them in such great depth that they molded history for generations.

You now know that it's all right to make a profit in life. It is your right and obligation. The purpose of that prosperity is to help others. It's not to be gained at the expense of others but in contribution to them. There's more than enough of everything that is good to go around. As you become a warrior with a heart of compassion, you'll realize that the counterfeit example that you've been given of selfishness and greed doesn't have to be your experience. You are called on to break the mold and give birth to a whole new set of ideas, concepts, and insights on how to conduct business and live out your life in the most optimal way.

Someone once said, "It's not how you start, it's how you finish that counts." Life is a collection of various kinds of experiences. Some of those experiences are great; others are not so great. However, all of the experiences that you have in life can work together for your ultimate good, if you learn the lessons they have to teach you. Compassionate samurai are in a continuous mode of learning, which means there's an allowance for mistakes—especially in the beginning.

When a baby is learning how to walk and she constantly falls, her parents don't berate her. They pick her up, caress her, tell her she's doing a good job, and allow her to keep trying until she gets it. With that same train of thought, you, too, must continue to apply the traits of a compassionate samurai so that you become more and more proficient. The road of a compassionate samurai is difficult. It is pockmarked with setbacks. They are not to be feared but embraced. Don't be afraid of the word *mastery*.

Please do not view mastery as an elusive goal that seems impossible to achieve. Mastery is simply proficiency in the application of these character traits in any circumstance through repetitive rehearsal. Mastery doesn't mean that you'll never have more to learn. You can always enhance your knowledge in any area, even in your areas of strength. This is all about going to the next level in life. The point is that you never really graduate. You only go from one level to the next.

In traditional aikido, there are only two belts offered: a white belt worn by those who are *kyu*-ranked *(mudansha)*, and a black belt worn by those who are *dan*-ranked *(yudansha)*. Unlike karate and tae kwon do, some people train in aikido for three to four years and still wear the white belt. For the average American sports enthusiast, it might appear as if this is a waste of time. In reality, the student is moving closer toward his or her goal after each class. The goal is not to wear a colorful belt or to get an award to hang on the wall. The goal is to master the art. The serious student is willing to put as much time in as necessary to achieve that end.

Mastery is not something that's hard to pin down, neither is it a vague concept. You're already a master in many areas. You can read. You've read this book to this point, which makes you a master of reading. That, of course, doesn't mean that you can't receive pointers here and there on how to become better at reading. It simply means that reading is something that's second nature to you. Putting on your clothes, bathing yourself, and making sure that you eat are all activities that are second nature to you.

You don't contemplate these activities. You just do them. Your subconscious mind, which is your greater mind, carries out these commands as natural functions of your everyday life. How does it know to do that? It's not as if you remind yourself how to read, eat, bathe, or take care of your personal health needs. You do it instinctively because you've repeated the process hundreds, maybe thousands, of times. If you want to create lasting change in your life, you will do it through repetition, emotional involvement, or a combination of both.

If you want to create lasting change in life, you will do it through repetition, emotional involvement, or a combination of both. Oh, did I just repeat that sentence?

You actually noticed that. Repetition and emotion are what brand character into your subconscious mind. It's not what you do every now and then that counts. It's what you're committed to do all the time that becomes your character. I know quite well that change can happen in an instant. However, lasting change happens over time through intentional repetitive action.

With that in mind, compassionate samurai are committed to making the traits not just a great read, but an everyday part of their lives. Through repetition, these ten traits will become your second nature. You will begin to think, feel, and act on them without having to think about it. Make a practice of reading parts of this book repetitively and commit the main points about each trait to memory. This chapter is meant to assist you in finding ways to put each trait into practice. I recommend that you focus on one trait every day for an entire week.

This system of repetition will ensure that you're working in depth. After each trait, I've listed a place for you to reflect and take action. What will you do to seize the opportunity to put each trait into action? The thing that you choose needs to become your focus and your binding agreement with yourself. If you have a hard time being true to yourself, then get a partner who will hold you accountable for following through on each of these traits. In ten weeks, you will have completed all the traits. Can you commit to doing that? *Will* you commit to doing that?

Commitment

The average person believes in doing what he says he's going to do only when conditions are optimal or conducive for keeping his word. But quite honestly, commitment doesn't have any conditions. Get in the habit of making commitments that may even be somewhat uncomfortable, and keep them. Sometimes you need to put yourself out there. If you're the kind of person who shies away from making commitment because you're afraid you won't follow through, then you need to make huge commitments and thrust all of your energy into making sure that you keep your commitment.

If you're the kind of person who overcommits, yet never follows through on all of the big commitments you proudly make, you may need to streamline your far-fetched goals down to bite-size commitments that you can deliver on. Make a few small promises and keep them. Build slowly on top of the previous commitment that you made. There's an adage that says "You are only as good as your word." I'd like to say, "You are only as good as the last word that you kept."

Exercise

On a separate piece of paper, complete the following:

- List three commitments that you should have made but that you put off.

- Describe your plan of action to follow through on your commitments.

- If you tend to overcommit, what were the last three commitments you made that you broke? Revisit each of those commitments. Why did you break them? And what did you receive in exchange for your broken commitment? What was the price that you paid for the broken commitment? What can you do now to begin making good on your commitment?

- List the last three commitments you made that you broke.

- Every day this week, keep a log of all the commitments you make and whether you've kept them or not. No commitment is too small to write down.

Personal Responsibility

Compassionate samurai choose to.
Average people have to.

Compassionate samurai believe that where they are in life—and where they are not—is directly connected to the choices they make. Average people take the *victim* viewpoint that life happens to them. Not only is life a collection of experiences, but it is also a compilation of all the choices you've made—both good and bad. In order to break the conventional mode of blaming others for why you haven't reached your goals, you have to become personally responsible.

Whether it's in your relationships, the kind of job you have, the income that you earn, or your education or lack thereof, you always have the ability to choose. You can always opt to take the personal responsibility route and drastically change your entire outcome. There's no such thing as being doomed to failure. You're only doomed to failure because that's the choice you made. You become defeated when you admit to defeat and deny that you have choices.

Think about Viktor Frankl's story. He could have chosen to avoid personal responsibility and become a product of the concentration camps. Had he chosen to succumb to his horrific environment, most people would not have judged him. In fact, most people would have felt sorry for him and wholeheartedly understood why he'd made such a decision. That didn't matter to Frankl. He chose to focus on the things that represented life in the most unassuming ways. He focused on his ability to choose his attitude and the value of life itself.

Maybe you're not as intentional as Viktor Frankl. I'll admit that he definitely had an inner strength that most people can't imagine. Regardless of whether you have his determination, you still have a remarkable ability to take personal responsibility for everything in your life. Just take a quick inventory, and make a list of everything that you want that is not present. Own the choices you've made. If something *is* in your life, it's because you've chosen for it to stay. If it's not in your life, it's because you haven't given it an invitation to enter. In the final analysis, it's all you—and that's being personally responsible.

Exercise

On a separate piece of paper, answer the following:

- In what areas of your life today did you play the blame game?

- Write down each time you felt you had to do something, and immediately say to yourself, "I choose to do this."

- What choice can you make today that will make a major difference in your life and in the life of one other person?

Contribution

> *Compassionate samurai give*
> *without thought of personal gain.*
> *Average people give when there is something in it*
> *for them and when it doesn't cost them too much.*

Let's make something clear: Giving to get isn't a bad thing. People do it every day, everywhere, and it works. You give your time to your employer with the expectation of receiving a paycheck at the end of the week. That is giving to get. At all levels of giving, there's always personal gain, even if that gain is a sense of satisfaction that you're helping others accomplish their dreams in life. A compassionate samurai gives without the thought of personal gain. It's not that personal gain won't come. You shall reap whatever you sow. The motivation for giving isn't centered on gain. This isn't an area that you're going to become an expert in overnight. This practice is definitely a higher truth to live by. You don't need wealth to operate at this high level. All you need to understand is that giving to get is good, but giving without the thought of getting is even better.

When you give on that level, you have mastery over your inner desires and tendencies toward greed and self-indulgence. There's no way you can stop the receptivity factor from taking place. When you give, that which you give will always come back to you on a grander scale. Warren Buffett made the single largest donation ever—$30.7 billion worth of shares in his Berkshire Hathaway corporation—to the Bill and Melinda Gates Foundation to help feed, clothe, shelter, educate, and provide health care for children and families in Africa.

Although Mr. Buffett doesn't need any more money, according to the law of sowing and reaping, billions of dollars are looking for him and his company right now. There's nothing he can do about that. It's a law. However, his motivation wasn't centered on self, but rather on helping people who really can't do anything to return the favor. That's when you know that you're giving on the highest level—when you give from your heart and don't expect a return from the person that you're giving to. You don't give to get. You give because you choose to be a giver.

Exercise

Each day of this week, focus on a different area of giving.

	AREAS WHERE YOU CAN GIVE	Whom did you give to and how?	Rate the difficulty of risk from 1–5
1. Encouragement			
2. Time			
3. Money			
4. Knowledge			
5. Your heart			

- What can you do today to jump-start your effort in becoming a major contributor to the good work of your choice?

Focus

> *Compassionate samurai anchor reality to their vision.*
> *Average people anchor their vision to reality.*

Focus is the ability to direct your attention, efforts, or activity at a desired direction or object without being distracted. Without a doubt, it's a quality that makes or breaks a compassionate samurai. It's the deciding factor of whether a samurai will ever achieve greatness in life. If I could summarize success, it would sound like this: *Success is the ability to not get distracted in life.* As simplistic as that may sound, it's really true. Your ability to focus on what you want will yield the desires of your heart.

Your capacity to focus on the benefits in life will far outweigh the process that you may have to endure in order to *receive* those benefits. My friend Bob Harrison always tells the story of David and Goliath. David, a scrawny teenage shepherd boy, was eager to battle the nine-foot giant named Goliath. Goliath was notorious for slaying entire armies with his strength alone. The young boy was no match for the skilled assassin. While others fled in fear from a giant they thought was too large to kill, David thought just the opposite: This giant was too large *not* to kill.

What made David fearless was that he focused on the rewards the king had promised to whoever killed Goliath: a beautiful woman, property, and freedom from taxes for life. When you focus on the benefits of life, you always get more benefits. When you focus on the problems, you'll inevitably get more problems. Compassionate samurai are disciplined to stay focused on the thing that they choose. Life will present you with multiple distractions. Your ability to ignore them will enable you to kill more giants than you've ever thought possible.

Exercise

On a separate piece of paper:

- Write a paragraph on your life's purpose. Why are you alive?

- Start each day with a list of the three most important things you need to accomplish.

- Each day write a paragraph about the biggest distraction that kept you from accomplishing your three most important things? Was it feelings? Other people? A habit?

Honesty

Compassionate samurai say what they mean and mean what they say. Average people are honest when it's convenient.

Honesty has become a lost virtue in the Western world. As old-fashioned as it may sound, honesty is still the best policy. At first it may seem as if you're getting away with being dishonest, but dishonesty will always catch up with you. Even when it's inconvenient and uncomfortable to do so, choose honesty. Trust is the foundation of all relationships. Honesty is the fuel that keeps all relationships moving forward.

Honesty is to a relationship as gasoline is to an automobile. A compassionate samurai chooses honesty all of the time. Some people try to qualify honesty. Some believe that certain situations require honesty, while other circumstances allow them to be dishonest. Honesty is simply communicating truth to the best of your ability and knowledge at all times.

Let's recap for a moment and look at the ways in which people try to disguise their dishonesty:

1. Telling somebody something that isn't so—
   this is the most blatant form. Here people
   choose to tell outright lies.

2. Giving the illusion of what is not so—this is
   a bit more clandestine in its approach. You're
   not telling an outright lie, but you're giving
   the illusion of something being true when in
   actuality it isn't.

3. Not telling what is so—many people fall into
   the category of not necessarily saying what isn't
   so, but not telling what is. The sun is not out
   tonight, but the moon is. Don't leave out the
   moon when it's quite obvious. Don't leave out
   information that will help give credence to your
   honest confession.

4. Pretending not to know—everyone knows about
   this game. If I pretend not to know and just don't
   confess, then nobody can ever accuse me of not
   being honest.

Exercise

Day 1: Write a page on what you pretended not to
know.

Day 2: Write a page on when you felt the need to
hold back the truth. When did you not say
what you meant?

Day 3: Write a page on when you didn't mean what you said.

Day 4: How transparent were you today? Where did it assist you and where did it hold you back?

Day 5: When were you vague to cover up the truth?

Honor

> *Compassionate samurai hold*
> *principles above personal benefit.*
> *Average people do whatever is best for themselves.*

Traditional samurai always display honor, even when dealing with their enemies. When one samurai kills another, he bows over the dead body of his slain opponent to show respect for the code that all samurai lived by. Our society is in dire need of people who will show others how to honor—no matter what. Children must honor their parents, not because their parents are perfect and can do no wrong, but because it's a principle that edifies all of humanity. Our willingness to honor the one who is entrusted to take care of us, protect us, and provide our daily needs forms a foundation of mutual respect.

Parents should honor their children. The first example a child has in life is his parents. The only basis for understanding how to properly honor other people comes from parents. If parents show little recognition and respect for their children, children will begin to show the same type of disrespect for their parents and others. Compassionate samurai encourage people with whom they come in contact to honor those who are in positions of authority. How we honor others is in direct relationship to how we view ourselves.

Make it a priority in front of your children, with people at work, and in society to always show honor toward other people. Honor people in high places, and honor people in the lowest strata of society. Just because someone is poor doesn't mean that you should discount him in any way. Just because an individual may be uneducated doesn't give you the right to show her dishonor. Show honor for your country. Many people tend to speak poorly about how things operate in the United States. Some people speak negatively about the United Kingdom or even Australia.

It's always bizarre that people can discredit the place where they choose to live. Remember personal responsibility: *You are where you are due to the choices you've made*. The truth is that you're living in a far better position than millions of people around the world. Things may not be exactly the way you want them to be, but they're optimal for your development and growth.

Three Areas of Honor to Always Remember

1. Honor whomever you interact with—you do not have to qualify those you honor. Honor isn't about status or fame. It's about how you view yourself. The level at which people disrespect others is directly connected to what they don't value within themselves.

2. Honor yourself—do not look down on yourself and your own efforts. You have as much to offer as others in society. It just looks different. There's a difference between positive esteem and conceit. You should feel very strong and positive about who you are and what you're becoming. Treat yourself like the king or queen that you are without holding it over people.

3. Always speak well of your mentors. What you say about them actually honors yourself. Your mentor's life is a sneak preview of where you're going in life. You can either accelerate your progress toward greatness or abort it all together by not honoring your mentor. Never speak disparagingly about your instructors. If you do, you'll cut yourself off from the source of much-needed direction for your journey.

Exercise

Day 1: Use listening as a way to honor people today and to record the impact you have.

Day 2: Write a paragraph on what honoring yourself would look like today. Can you do it?

Day 3: See if you can honor ten people today by edifying them in language to others.

Day 4: Honor three people today by soliciting their opinion.

Day 5: Make a list of your actions at work today and how they either honored or dishonored your co-workers.

Trust

Compassionate samurai have the capacity to trust others and themselves with their life and the wisdom to know when to do so.

Average people are either unwilling to trust others to be as trustworthy as they are or trust blindly without doing due diligence.

Trust takes time to build and can be lost in a moment. Have you ever watched a skyscraper being built? The process is pretty amazing. It often takes more than one year just to prepare and set the foundation for the building. In some cases, it actually takes longer to prepare and build the foundation than it takes to erect the physical structure. That is because the strength of the foundation determines how strong the building will be once it's erected. The taller the building is, the deeper the foundation must be. This same building concept can be seen with regard to building trust.

When a person first meets you, she will probably have limited trust in you since you've given her no experience to form trust. Wise people don't trust just anyone. First, people give their trust to other people with whom they're interested in developing a relationship on some level. That relationship could be a business relationship, a marital relationship, a friendship, a partnership, and so on. Trust is based on a person's desire to build a relationship. You don't even have to be a friend of another person to feel that your trust has been betrayed.

If the President of the United States committed a crime against the people and violated the oath he had sworn to uphold, most Americans would feel that their trust had been weakened. Trust isn't just about personal involvement. It's about the integrity of a person's words and deeds. Once trust is broken, it's difficult to rebuild. A skyscraper may have taken a year or two to be built, but it can be destroyed by dynamite in a matter of seconds. Broken trust has the same effect.

If you have broken trust, there's still hope, but it will take time and much effort to restore what was taken for granted. The skyscraper can be rebuilt, but the process will take just as long as it did the first time. It may take even longer, considering the debris that must be cleared before the new job is started. Compassionate samurai know this and live by the code of trust at all times.

Exercise

Day 1: Look for three ways that you can display your trust in others today. Perhaps it is giving them the authority to make a decision.

Day 2: Look for three ways you can display trust in yourself today.

Day 3: What task can you tackle today that will help you increase trust in yourself? It should be one that tests your capability.

Day 4: Have an open conversation with someone who has violated your trust. After expressing your fears and concerns, negotiate a task he or she can do to rebuild a piece of your trust.

Day 5: Have an open conversation with someone whose trust you've violated. Was the breakdown a spoken or unspoken expectation or agreement? After conveying your feelings, make an agreement that begins to restore the original broken agreement.

Abundance

> *Compassionate samurai ask, "How can I?"*
> *Average people ask, "Can I?"*

Abundance is the viewpoint that your wholeness and completeness don't depend on external circumstances. Scarcity is the viewpoint that there isn't enough and is usually based on the person feeling that he or she is not enough.

Abundance is more than something that you have or do. Abundance is a way of thinking—it's a lifestyle. To become proficient in a particular language, you have to think in that language until it becomes a part of you. To be abundant, you have to think abundance all of the time. Because of your connection to an infinite God, you are whole and complete. Because He is infinite, you have unlimited resources. That means that you never entertain scarcity even when you're in circumstances that appear scarce.

The scarcity mind-set says that there's not enough to go around, so you have to hoard the little you have for fear of losing it. Further, if you lose what you have, you won't be able to recover, since there's so little in the world to go around. Abundance says that there's more than enough for everyone. With abundance thinking, compassionate samurai look for ways to expand the pie, rather than worrying about how much of the pie they'll get. A major way to identify whether you're living with abundance thinking is by evaluating yourself. Ask yourself, *Do I always feel as though I have more than enough to share with others?* If so, you are operating with abundance thinking.

Exercise

1. How can you operate from abundance with regard to time today? Spend 15 minutes looking for ways to leverage your time to solve something you didn't think you had time to do.

2. Operate today from an abundance of love and self-esteem. Keep a log of when you felt rejected to any degree. Can you act as if you have an infinite amount of love, friends, or customers? Record your experiences.

3. Operate today from financial abundance. Give an amount of money that is a stretch for you to a person in need. Buy someone lunch. Spend 15 minutes coming up with ways to generate additional income.

4. Identify where you see a limited number of ways of doing something, whether it's completing your work for the day or buying a home. Force yourself to ask, "How can I solve this in another way?" Operate today from a solution orientation. Record your experiences.

5. Operate today from an abundance of energy. If you had twice the energy, what would you do? Now think about how you can do it. Record your experiences.

Boldness

> *Compassionate samurai ask,*
> *"What will happen if I don't take this risk?"*
> *Average people ask, "What will happen if I fail?"*

For compassionate samurai, courage isn't optional. It's the creed they live by each day. They are always looking for situations to display boldness and to take risks. They don't back away from risk-taking opportunities; they embrace the opportunities. They're not afraid of death and dying because they already consider themselves dead. That is what creates a totally new level of boldness in them, knowing that they have nothing to lose. This doesn't mean they're reckless with their life. Compassionate samurai value life and play full-out. Compassionate samurai see life in terms of what the consequences will be if they don't do something.

The spice of life for compassionate samurai rests in each opportunity to display courage. A traditional samurai knew that he wasn't like everyone else. His life assignment was different. He knew that he was different. For him, showing off his skills wasn't courageous. He was courageous with a cause. He was being called to do more for the greater good of humanity.

Courageous people get the best that life has to offer because they make demands that the fearful are too afraid to make. Life doesn't give to those who deserve it. We all deserve better things in life! Life gives to those who are bold enough to *demand* their rightful inheritance.

Exercise

Day 1: Have a courageous conversation with a co-worker or boss. Write about your experience.

Day 2: What risky project can you take on at work today?

Day 3: What is a risk for you in your personal life? Are you willing to take it on today? Write about your experience whether you do it or not.

Day 4: How many times and in how many ways can you risk being wrong today?

Day 5: How many times and in how many ways can you risk looking foolish today?

Knowledge

Compassionate samurai are satisfied without being settled.
Average people are settled without being satisfied.

Always adopt a beginner's mind-set. No matter who you are or how much you think you know in life, there's always more for you to learn. It's not about your college degree. That has its place, and I encourage everyone to get a quality education. However, the knowledge that you must always seek is that which makes you more, which increases and adds value to your character. I've always been a bit nervous about people who believe they know everything. These people are dangerous because they're blind to receiving help.

No one knows everything. You can learn from the most unassuming person. Children are often the greatest teachers for how to live life to the fullest and how to forgive and move on. Compassionate samurai dedicate their entire lives to learning and increasing their knowledge and the wisdom to apply it. With regard to knowledge, a compassionate samurai never "arrives." There's always more to learn, more to discover, and more to live.

Compassionate samurai do not settle for good. Good can be an enemy to great. If compassionate samurai have to choose between good and great, they always choose great. But greatness is never achieved by accident, and it's never free. Greatness in all forms is intentional. Michael Jordan was great at basketball because he relentlessly pursued ways to exploit his talents and was willing to pay the price of time, energy, and a beginner's mind. Bill Gates is great at computer software applications because he relentlessly pursues ways to improve and is willing to pay the price of time, energy, and a beginner's mind.

Compassionate samurai are able to maintain this relentless pursuit of everything getting better without feeling that it's not enough, because their satisfaction is in alignment with their purpose. Since they have no resistance to the way things are, they're free to devote all their energy to creation. Compassionate samurai are clear that they're already "whole and complete," and they create games of "more and better" to assist in the process of creation.

This is the kind of knowledge that you must embrace. It is the mind-set that keeps you clearly beyond any of your competitors. Don't misconstrue the message here. This isn't about competition for the sake of being competitive. This competition is for you, a compassionate samurai, to be all that you can be.

Exercise

Day 1: Take 15 minutes and write down all the areas in which you've been settling for the good you have instead of producing the next level of greatness. Look at your job, your relationships with your co-workers, your marriage, your health, your spiritual growth, and everything else that comes to mind. Pick one area where you're specifically committed to a spectacular level of achievement.

Day 2: Identify one area you consider yourself an expert in. Approach three people who may not have your level of expertise and challenge yourself to be so open that you receive valued insight from them.

Day 3: Identify one area in which you've confused your results with who you are. This is an area where your self-esteem suffers because you don't have the results you want. This could be your weight, the quality of a relationship, a job performance review, and so on. Write down the phrase *This is it and I'm satisfied.* Write how nonresistance to this circumstance looks different from resignation. Spend ten minutes looking at how this circumstance could be in alignment with your purpose.

Day 4: Look for one discussion today where you had to be right. Write a page on how you might have had the same discussion outside the right/wrong paradigm without giving up your viewpoint.

Day 5: What area of knowledge would make the most significant difference in the pursuit of your purpose? Write a page on your system to increase your knowledge in this area over the next month. Is it to interview an expert a week? Is it to read 20 minutes, five days a week? Commit to a system. Without a system, very little sustained change occurs.

Commit these traits to memory. Live them with conviction. Live life not by accident, but on purpose. Finish strong!

ACKNOWLEDGMENTS

First, I would like to recognize all of the compassionate samurai who have dedicated their careers to conducting, facilitating, and helping to promote Klemmer & Associates Leadership Seminars all over the world. They conscientiously live their lives by very high standards and principles, which benefits others and also themselves. Their example helped to provide the depth in the pages of this book, making it a continual, living, work-in-progress rather than simply words on a piece of paper. They did not ask to be recognized. Their only appeal was to you, the reader, to live your life on a much higher level as a result of reading this work. There are a few compassionate samurai I am proud to call friends who are ordinary people doing extraordinary things.

1. Jim Stovall (**www.theultimategift.org**)
2. Bob Harrison (**www.increase.org**)
3. Azim Khamisa (**www.tkf.org**)

A special thanks goes to my parents Ken and Alice Klemmer. To my wife of 22 years, Roma Klemmer, for her never-ending support. And, I thank my children for living up to the high expectations on them. A very special thanks goes to Dr. Aaron D. Lewis for his writing and rewriting of this material. To the team at Hay House for seeing the value in publishing this book, realizing its potential to touch numerous lives in a positive way.

There are many more people too numerous to mention, but without whom this book would not have been written. Being surrounded by so many compassionate samurai, I know that I am truly blessed.

∞

Recommended Reading

Cleary, Thomas. 1999. *Code of the Samurai: A Modern Translation of the Bushido Shoshinshu of Taira Shigesuke*. North Clarendon, VT: Charles E. Tuttle Co.

Frankl, Viktor. 1977. *Man's Search for Meaning*. New York: Pocket.

Goldratt, Eliyahu M. 1999. *Theory of Constraints*. North Barrington, MA: North River Press.

Gutteridge, Rene. 2007. *The Ultimate Gift* (movie edition with promotional CD). Nashville: Westbow Press.

Kegan, Robert and Lisa Laskow Lahey. 2001. *How the Way We Talk Can Change the Way We Work*. San Francisco: Jossey-Bass.

Klemmer, Brian. 2006. *Eating the Elephant One Bite at a Time*. Tulsa: Insight.

———2005. *If How-To's Were Enough, We Would All Be Skinny, Rich & Happy*. Tulsa: Insight.

———2004. *When Good Intentions Run Smack Into Reality: Twelve Lessons to Coach Yourself and Others to Peak Performance*. Tulsa: Insight.

Leonard, George. 1999. *The Way of Aikido: Life Lessons from an American Sensei*. Plume: New York.

———1992. *Mastery: The Keys to Success and Long Term Fulfillment*. Plume: New York.

Munroe, Myles. 2000. *The Burden of Freedom*. Lake Mary, FL: Creation House.

Stovall, Jim. 1991. *The Ultimate Gift*. Colorado Springs: River Oak.

Thurman, Howard. 1963. *Disciplines of the Spirit*. New York: Harper & Row.

Trump, Donald and Robert Kiyosaki. 2006. *Why We Want You to Be Rich: Two Men One Message*. Scottsdale: Rich Press.

Twist, Lynne. 2003. *The Soul of Money: Transforming Your Relationship with Money and Life*. New York: W. W. Norton.

Welch, Jack and Suzy Welch. 2005. *Winning*. New York: Harper Collins.

About the Author

Brian Klemmer has studied leadership since graduating from the United States Military Academy (1968–1972). He's the author of the best-selling books *If How-To's Were Enough, We Would All Be Skinny, Rich, & Happy; When Good Intentions Run Smack into Reality;* and *Eating the Elephant One Bite at a Time.* Known for his humorous and practical style of communicating, Brian is one of today's most in-demand speakers.

His character development and leadership seminar company, Klemmer & Associates Leadership Seminars, Inc., has conducted its work for more than 100,000 people around the world, influencing those in countries such as the U.S., Saudi Arabia, Australia, Mexico, Spain, the Philippines, and Scandinavia. Brian's clients includes well-known corporations such as Aetna Life Insurance, American Suzuki Corporation, General Electric, Walt Disney Attractions, and distributors for more than a dozen network-marketing and direct-sales organizations.

Klemmer and Associates seminars measure and produce long lasting changes in people; and you can find out more about them by visiting them online at **www.klemmer.com** or by calling (800) 577-5447.

NOTES

NOTES

NOTES

NOTES

NOTES

NOTES

NOTES

NOTES

We hope you enjoyed this Hay House book.
If you'd like to receive our online catalog featuring additional
information on Hay House books and products, or if you'd like to
find out more about the Hay Foundation, please contact:

Hay House, Inc.
P.O. Box 5100
Carlsbad, CA 92018-5100

(760) 431-7695 or **(800) 654-5126**
(760) 431-6948 (fax) or **(800) 650-5115 (fax)**
www.hayhouse.com® • **www.hayfoundation.org**

Published and distributed in Australia by: Hay House Australia Pty.
Ltd., 18/36 Ralph St., Alexandria NSW 2015 • *Phone:* 612-9669-4299 •
Fax: 612-9669-4144 • www.hayhouse.com.au

Published and distributed in the United Kingdom by: Hay House UK,
Ltd., 292B Kensal Rd., London W10 5BE • *Phone:* 44-20-8962-1230 •
Fax: 44-20-8962-1239 • www.hayhouse.co.uk

Published and distributed in the Republic of South Africa by:
Hay House SA (Pty), Ltd., P.O. Box 990, Witkoppen 2068 • *Phone/Fax:*
27-11-467-8904 • www.hayhouse.co.za

Published in India by: Hay House Publishers India, Muskaan Complex,
Plot No. 3, B-2, Vasant Kunj, New Delhi 110 070 • *Phone:* 91-11-4176-
1620 • *Fax:* 91-11-4176-1630 • www.hayhouse.co.in

Distributed in Canada by: Raincoast, 9050 Shaughnessy St., Vancouver,
B.C. V6P 6E5 • *Phone:* (604) 323-7100 • *Fax:* (604) 323-2600
www.raincoast.com

Take Your Soul on a Vacation

Visit **www.HealYourLife.com®** to regroup, recharge, and reconnect
with your own magnificence.Featuring blogs, mind-body-spirit news,
and life-changing wisdom from Louise Hay and friends.

Visit **www.HealYourLife.com** today!

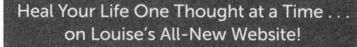